Turn Up the Volume

Turn Up the Volume equips journalism students, professionals, and others interested in producing audio content with the know-how necessary to launch a podcast for the first time. It addresses the unique challenges beginner podcasters face in producing professional level audio for online distribution. Beginners can learn how to handle the technical and conceptual challenges of launching, editing, and posting a podcast.

This book exposes readers to various techniques and formats available in podcasting. It includes the voices of industry experts as they recount their experiences producing their own podcasts and podcast content. It also examines how data analytics can help grow an audience and provide strategies for marketing and monetization. Written accessibly, *Turn Up the Volume* gives you a clear and detailed path to launching your first podcast.

Michael O'Connell is one of the founders and host of the podcast *It's All Journalism*. O'Connell presents to journalists around the country about beginning and sustaining new podcasts. He is also the Senior Digital Editor at Federal News Radio in Washington, DC.

Turn Up the Volume

Volume

A Down and Dirty Guide
to Podcasting

Michael O'Connell

Routledge
Taylor & Francis Group
NEW YORK AND LONDON

First published 2017
by Routledge
711 Third Avenue, New York, NY 10017

and by Routledge
2 Park Square, Milton Park, Abingdon, Oxon, OX14 4RN

Routledge is an imprint of the Taylor & Francis Group, an informa business

© 2017 Taylor & Francis

Library of Congress Cataloging-in-Publication Data
Names: O'Connell, Michael, 1961– author.
Title: Turn up the volume : a down and dirty guide to podcasting / Michael O'Connell.
Description: New York, NY : Routledge, 2017. | Includes bibliographical references.
Identifiers: LCCN 2017004176 | ISBN 9781138218024 (hardback) | ISBN 9781138218031 (pbk.)
Subjects: LCSH: Podcasting.
Classification: LCC TK5105.887 .O34 2017 | DDC 006.7/876—dc23
LC record available at https://lccn.loc.gov/2017004176

ISBN: 978-1-138-21802-4 (hbk)
ISBN: 978-1-138-21803-1 (pbk)
ISBN: 978-1-315-43876-4 (ebk)

Typeset in Warnock Pro
by Apex CoVantage, LLC

Visit the companion website: www.routledge.com/cw/oconnell

For Fran, the love of my life and my inspiration.

Contents

Preface   ix
Acknowledgments   xvi
Introduction   xviii

1 The Tenets of Good Podcasting   1

2 Setting Up Your Studio   21

3 Preparing for Your First Episode   40

4 Turn Your Ideas into Audio   62

5 Bring the World into Your Podcast   78

6 Editing: Pulling All the Pieces Together   90

7 Where Will Your Podcast Live Online?   109

8 Growing and Sustaining Your Podcast   124

Appendix A: Music Rights, Incorporation and Other
   Legal Considerations   151
Appendix B: Shopping Guide   163
Appendix C: It's All Journalism Questionnaire   166

Bibliography   *168*
Resources   *171*
Glossary   *174*
Index   *180*

Preface

Podcasts are about storytelling.

So, here's my story.

In 2010, I was a 49-year-old journalist trapped in a job I hated.

That wasn't always the case. As the managing editor of four weekly news-papers in northern Virginia, I had the privilege of working with a team of creative people reporting the news and serving four diverse communities. The work was occasionally challenging and often fulfilling.

Two things, though, disrupted the newspaper industry in the first decade of the 21st century.

FIGURE 0.1 Michael O'Connell is the co-host of *It's All Journalism* and the author of "Turn Up the Volume."

As it had altered nearly every aspect of daily life, the arrival of the internet triggered a huge upheaval in newsrooms across the country.

Readers suddenly had access to an unlimited stream of news, which, on the surface, was not a bad thing. You could get up-to-the-minute scores from your favorite baseball team or read in-depth reports about the latest happenings on Capitol Hill.

There were even "citizen journalists"—new, free voices, unaffiliated with any news outlets—sharing their fresh perspectives with an online audience.

Don't get me wrong. More information for more people coming from more voices is a good thing. In fact, it's a great, positive thing for a democratic society.

The problem was that digital technology gutted the economic structures that propped up legacy news outlets.

People didn't need to purchase a classified ad to sell their old mattress and box springs. They could list it for free on Craigslist. Why should a furniture store pay so much for a display ad in a weekly newspaper when it could run the ad on its own website?

Suddenly, the press, the traditional gatekeepers of the news, faced a dilemma. On one hand, the internet solved the costly distribution problem. Rather than wait for a publisher to report, write, edit, print and ship a physical product to their doorsteps, readers could access a newspaper's content online.

But, although all that content was available at everybody's fingertips 24 hours a day, seven days a week, readers proved less inclined to monetarily support the news outlets or their advertisers. Sure, there were online ads and paywalls, but why pay for access to a website when you could follow a social media link that gives you a backdoor to the story or read a similar or aggregated story elsewhere for free?

And online ads? Ad blockers will keep those pesky things out of your face altogether.

The media industry, by and large, failed to act quickly enough to offset this upheaval. With media revenue streams drying up, cities that were once two-paper towns became one-paper or—worse—no-paper towns. Across the

U.S., between 2003 and 2013, newspaper newsrooms cut their staffs by nearly one-third.[1] Journalists, many with decades of experience, were out of work.

The second disruption occurred with the recession of 2008. Now it wasn't just newspapers that were struggling; all segments of the economy were hit. People lost their homes. Companies went out of business. Families everywhere suffered.

In that environment, two years later, when I was contemplating how much I hated my job, I had to count my blessings.

At least I had a job when many journalists did not. We owned our home. My wife worked for a government contractor, and we lived in the nearly recession-proof Washington, DC, area.

The news company that I worked for, a chain of local weeklies, was surviving—barely. Small advertisers still needed an outlet for their ads, but even those mom-and-pop shops spent less and less money.

To offset the shrinking revenue, the company cut wages and staff, stopped filling positions as people left, and even shrank the page size and page count of the papers themselves. Editions that once boasted 48 pages of local news every week now published 16 or 12 pages of content, some of which was repurposed over multiple communities.

The result of this hang-on-at-any-cost approach created an uncomfortable environment, where I was working harder than I ever had on a product with which I was becoming progressively less satisfied.

I hated it, in fact. I felt trapped.

At this point, at age 49, I did something I'd never done before. I asked myself, "Where do you want to be in five years?"

I didn't want to be where I was; I knew that. But I still wanted to be a journalist. I loved telling stories and reporting the news.

It was clear to me that, in five years, print journalism would probably be in just as bad a shape if not worse. Despite the disruption in the industry caused by the internet, that's where the journalism jobs would be. That's where *I* needed to be.

The American University's School of Communications in Washington offered a two-year, weekends only, Master's in Interactive Journalism program. It was a perfect fit. Sixty intense, eight-hour classes hyper-focused on digital storytelling. It changed my life.

What I liked most about AU's Interactive Journalism program were the guest speakers. These were working journalists who shared stories of innovation in their newsrooms. I would drive home each Saturday afternoon, my head on fire with ideas and inspiration. I was excited about journalism again.

About this time, I began listening to podcasts during my commute. I subscribed mostly to entertainment shows, like comedian and TV host Chris Hardwick's *The Nerdist* and writer-director Kevin Smith's *SModcast*.

Those shows in particular proselytized about the strengths of the medium, in particular its do-it-yourself, get-a-mic-and-make-a-podcast aesthetic.

As I drove to class one Saturday morning, I said to myself, "I should do a podcast."

The more I thought about it, the more it made sense. "I should do a podcast about journalism, about how it's changing and how I see things differently now as I'm changing the direction of my career."

"There must be other journalists, like me, feeling trapped, confused, angry, lost, betrayed by the industry they loved. I should do a podcast for them."

The road to the launch of that podcast, what would become *It's All Journalism*, took a meandering path.

I switched jobs, joining one of my classmates, Jolie Lee, on the digital team at Federal News Radio in DC. Our sister station, WTOP, hired another classmate, Megan Cloherty, to work on its news team.

After graduation in May 2012, the three of us talked a lot about doing a podcast and swapped ideas for potential guests.

But how do you do a podcast, anyway? The problem with the DIY approach is it's all down to you in the end.

Working at a radio station solved one of the big problems—access to a studio where we could record and edit. We had guests and topics, and we could do interviews, but what do you do with the audio when you're done editing it? Where do you post it? How does it live online? How do you post it on iTunes? How do you get people to listen to it or care that it exists?

DIY or not, we needed to talk to somebody who could answer those questions.

Back at my old newspaper job, I had interviewed Carolyn Belefski, a local cartoonist who published the online comic strip *Curls*. She and her husband, Joe Carabeo, recorded a weekly podcast, *The Carolyn and Joe Show*, in their living room. I met with them at a coffee shop and picked their brains about podcasting.

Joe, a talented photographer and filmmaker, took care of the production end of their podcast. He explained their recording setup and how he posted the podcast online.

They both talked about the importance of posting regularly and how they'd made the podcast a part of their weekly routine. They also discussed structuring a podcast around topics of interest and regular segments, such as "Carolyn's News," an update of their convention appearances and projects they were working on.

FIGURE 0.2 Carolyn Belefski and Joe Carabeo are hosts of *The Carolyn and Joe Show.*

All this provided valuable information as we prepared *It's All Journalism* for its launch, which finally took place Aug. 22, 2012.

Four years and more than 200 episodes later, I'm still learning about podcasting. We made a lot of mistakes along the way, but we had many successes as well. Jolie and Megan moved on, and other producers came and went. Despite all the changes, we never missed a week.

The thing no one tells you about podcasting is just how much work is involved in producing a weekly show. *It's All Journalism* is made up of interviews, so we're constantly hunting down guests, juggling schedules, doing research, writing, recording, editing and promoting. The work never really ends.

It occurred to me at some point that it would be helpful to others if I shared some of the lessons I've learned about producing a podcast. Occasionally, I'd blog about it on our website and make presentations at journalism conferences. This book, "Turn Up the Volume: A Down and Dirty Guide to Podcasting," is the result of those initial efforts.

If you're thinking about doing a podcast, stop thinking about it and just do it.

If you have the opportunity to take part in a creative endeavor, whether it's a podcast or something else, you will always discover something of value, usually unexpected, from the effort. You may not make a million dollars or garner thousands of followers on Twitter, but you will be enriched. I guarantee it.

A word about the book: I'm a journalist, so the only way I know how to tell a story is to talk to people and report what they said. I've got my own experiences, which I'll share here and there, but "Turn Up the Volume" is the culmination of a lot of conversations with podcasters, producers, broadcasting executives, podcasting platform chiefs, advertising experts and marketing personnel. I've tried to include as many voices in the book as possible.

Just like I sought out Joe and Carolyn to find out how to do my own podcast, I've talked to a variety of people in the podcasting industry—yes, we can probably call it an industry now—about what you need to know in order to successfully launch and grow a podcast. Take what you see as valuable and build on it.

Good luck.
Michael O'Connell
November 2016

NOTE

1 Jurkowitz, Mark (2014, March 26). "The Losses in Legacy." *State of the Media* (blog), Pew Research Center. [http://www.journalism.org/2014/03/26/the-losses-in-legacy]

Acknowledgments

Projects like this one are not executed without a great deal of help, support and patience from many people.

First, I'd like to thank all those who allowed me to interview them for the book. Not only were they generous with their time and expertise, but their enthusiasm for the project helped make the research process a joy from beginning to end. In particular, I'd like to thank Kevin Goldberg, who was both a source and quasi-editor for the section on music and legal issues.

I'd like to thank Carolyn Belefski and Joe Carabeo, both for the advice they gave me before I launched my podcast (*It's All Journalism*) and for their encouragement with this project. It was a pleasure to get Carolyn involved as the book's illustrator as well.

Thank you to Deb Cobb, who spent a strange two hours with me in a studio taking my book photo while I explained the process of launching a podcast to a fledgling podcaster. The picture came out well, considering the subject matter.

In addition, I want to say a big "thank you" to all the people at Federal News Radio, who were supportive of my podcasting and this strange part-time job that was taking up all my free time. A special thanks goes to my boss, Lisa Wolfe, who allowed me to focus on the book when I needed to and let me use Federal News Radio's facilities to record *It's All Journalism* and the interviews for this book.

I'm also grateful for the help of my editors at Taylor and Francis, Nicole Salazar and Ross Wagenhofer, who ably shepherded me through this project. Ross gets an extra thank-you for helping land me this opportunity. I never imagined I would have a chance to write a textbook. It's surprising what happens when you put yourself out there.

One of the promises I made myself when I decided to take on this project was to continue doing the weekly podcast throughout the writing process.

I'm happy to say that I was able to meet that goal, mostly thanks to the assistance of fellow producers Amber Healy and Nicole Ogrysko. Thanks for all the hard work, guys. Amber also gets a special shout-out as the copyeditor of "Turn Up The Volume." She wielded a wicked editing pencil. I'm forever grateful for her work on the project and her friendship.

None of this could have been done without the love and support of my family. My children and my wife, Fran, put up with quite a lot because of "the book." Even though I was a million miles away as I typed onto my laptop at the kitchen table, I was always aware of your proximity and the sacrifices you made in letting me "just work." Thank you. Thank you. Thank you.

Introduction

If you've been following the media for the last few years, interest in podcasting seems to be resurging.

Podcast listenership has grown steadily since Edison Research began studying the medium as part of its Infinite Dial measurement of media consumption in the United States.

In 2006, just 11 percent of the total U.S. population over the age of 12 said they listened to podcasts. Ten years later, in 2016, that figure had rocketed to 36 percent—an estimated 98 million people—according to Edison's June 2016 report. Monthly listenership grew from 9 percent in 2008 to 21 percent in 2016, with 13 percent—an estimated 35 million people—describing themselves as weekly podcast listeners.[1]

"I would say with the exception of this most recent year, it [growth in listenership]'s been linear and steady but not explosive," said Tom Webster, Edison's vice president of strategy and marketing.[2]

Compared to other forms of online audio media, podcasting's uptick hasn't been as steep as, say, that of Pandora or Spotify, which have displayed a sharp growth curve over the past six years.

"Podcasting has never really done that," Webster said. "It's been slow and linear, and I think it has really just been this past year where we've seen a really sharp uptick in growth. I mean, that difference from 17 percent to 21 percent is a 24 percent rise, and that's the sharpest that we've seen in the 11 or 12 years that we tracked it."[3]

Webster pointed to several factors as contributing to podcasting's sudden growth.

"One is there's heightened awareness of the medium, and I think *Serial* did that to some extent," he said. "Although *Serial* was really two years ago and didn't produce that kind of pop in its first year, it has made people aware of the term more. And so that's definitely part of it."[4]

Debuting in October 2014, the *Serial* podcast examined in detail the 1999 murder of Hae Min Lee in Baltimore, Maryland. Over its 12-episode first season, *Serial* brought into question the conviction of Lee's former boy-friend, Adnan Masud Syed. Each week, host Sarah Koenig meticulously reviewed the facts of the case, combining the best aspects of investigative journalism and long-form, serialized storytelling to engage the audience.[5]

Serial's popularity garnered a great deal of press coverage not only about Syed's case but also about the medium in general. *Serial* quickly shot to the top of the iTunes rankings, and, as of February 2016, its episodes have been downloaded 80 million times.[6] It also received a 2015 Peabody Award, for which it was called "an audio game-changer."[7]

A second factor in podcasting's growth was greater adoption of technology to ease consumer consumption.

"Mobile has continued to have a pretty big role here, because in the early days of podcasting, for many, many years, there was some friction in the process," Webster said. "You had to download the show to a hard drive and then you had to sync it to an iPod or possibly an iPhone to listen to later."[8]

Now, with a smartphone in your pocket and easy access to 4G, LTE or Wi-Fi, downloading an episode is just a click away.

"It's turned it into more of an impulse buy for a lot of people such that you're able to just say, 'Oh, I'd like to listen to this show now.' Click on the show and listen to it without any forethought or friction," Webster said.[9]

Ease of access helped the burgeoning listener base access an ever-widening variety of content, well beyond the 80 million downloads that *Serial* gar-nered. Apple announced in 2013 that podcast subscriptions on iTunes had surpassed 1 billion, with 250,000 unique podcasts available in 100 different languages.[10]

"I think content was really led by public media [such as NPR] who had a lot of great spoken word content anyway," Webster said. "But now as we've started to see investment in very high-level content, very top-quality content, you have this new tier of players—PodcastOne, Gimlet, Panoply, Midroll. They're essentially bringing a lot more kind of 'mainstream mass appeal' content into the space, so that may be the biggest driver of them all."[11]

One of the people banking on the medium's potential is Norm Pattiz, chief executive officer and founder of PodcastOne, a network that boasts a lineup of popular podcasts, including *The Adam Carolla Show*, *The Steve Austin Show Unleashed* and *Talk Is Jericho*. Before jumping into the podcasting space, Pattiz was the founder and former chairman of the Westwood One syndicated radio network.

Pattiz draws parallels between his experience at Westwood One and the fact that two-thirds of Americans have consumed a podcast.

"It means the same thing that happened to Westwood One in syndicated network radio, which was starting out as a $200,000 company in revenues

FIGURE 0.3 Norman Pattiz is the CEO and founder of PodcastOne.

and years thereafter becoming a $600 million revenue-generating machine and a public company with a $4 billion market cap 20 years ago," he said. "It means that from my perspective the opportunities are very much the same.

"When you take a look at the growth pattern of a company like PodcastOne, and you compare it to the growth pattern of a company like Westwood One, when we first started out radio was pretty much all local, and network and syndication weren't large parts of it. When you take a look at our growth pattern, they're almost identical. You don't have to be a rocket scientist to realize that what's happening in video already . . . is going to happen in audio as well."[12]

PodcastOne's model, which networks like Acast and Midroll are also using, revolves around stringing together a group of podcasts with large audiences and then using dynamic insertion to drop commercials within podcast episodes, allowing podcasting networks to sell advertising at scale. Niche content can be used for targeted advertising—for example, golf clubs being sold on a golf-themed podcast—or the audience from the entire network can be leveraged to sell big-ticket corporate sponsorships, such as by automobile or mattress manufacturers.

"Comparing digital to the broadcast medium today is sort of like comparing a six-shooter to an automatic weapon," Pattiz said. "We just have more things at our disposal. We can be much more granular in describing our audience. We can be much more granular in determining who's listening, where they're listening from and how long they're listening."[13]

These advantages are not only appealing to advertisers but attractive to content producers as well.

"I've talked to every major talent agency in the business, because those are people that I've done business with forever and they need digital solutions for their client base," Pattiz said. "It's not enough to just be talking about movies and TV in the traditional sense and record deals and publishing deals and what have you. They [the talent agencies] need to be in things that are digital, and their clients are more interested in wanting to own content than just be paid for doing it. Those are all things that we offer."[14]

With hundreds of thousands of podcasts being produced over an unlimited number of channels, the potential for growth is huge, but there are still hurdles to overcome.

"In some ways, you can see that is a wonderful opportunity, and we do too," said Brendan Monaghan, chief executive officer of Panoply. "But it's also a challenge, and it's not a commonly used medium yet. It's obviously growing considerably, but it's almost like the industry needs to have a 'Got Milk' campaign, just because there's just people who don't know about it or understand it yet. They carry around a device that has the podcast natively built into it— they just don't know what it does or how to use it. So I think that's one issue."[15]

Podcasting right now is big, and it's about to get bigger. Its audience has been growing steadily for 10 years. More people are listening, and more podcasts are being made to feed that demand. Big companies are lining up to take the medium to the next level, with the goal of making podcasting not just sustainable but profitable and as ubiquitous as TV or radio.

Yet, this was not always the case. In all the excitement around podcasting's apparent resurgence, it's easy to forget that it's a relatively new medium.

Guglielmo Marconi patented his radio wave transmission system in 1896, and a year later he launched the first commercial radio station.[16] Television developed in Europe and North America over the first few decades of the 20th century. It wasn't until after World War II, though, that it became the dominant form of mass communication that it is today.

Podcasting is not just radio on the internet. It was born there. It can trace its roots back to 1999, when two developers at Netscape, Dan Libby and Ramanathan V. Guha, released the first version of the Rich Site Summary (RSS), sometimes called Really Simple Syndication. This aggregation application allowed users to subscribe to a website and receive updates every time a website added new content. The process was entirely automatic. This freed the user from having to log on to a website to search for new content. All the user had to do was identify what they were interested in, subscribe to the RSS feed and then wait for updates.[17]

The early versions of RSS were text based. It would take the input of someone with a background in mass communications to push along the idea that RSS could be used to aggregate non-text content.

Enter former MTV veejay Adam Curry.

"It really started in 2000," Curry said. "I had moved back from the States, back to Europe. I was kind of looking around at stuff that was going on, and cable modems had just started. And the thing about the cable modem was not so much that we really didn't have super high bandwidth, but, in fact, it was being sold at the time as an always-on internet connection."[18]

With a background in traditional mainstream media, Curry was familiar with how content was created and distributed. Although the nightly news, for example, might describe itself as "live," it's actually made up of taped reports that are assembled and sent out over the broadcast each night. The content, some of which may be days old, is just waiting around for the moment when viewers can watch it.

The experience back then of audio and video consumption over the internet was quite poor by comparison.

"Even just for listening to an MP3, it was click, wait, wait, wait, and then it would start to play," Curry said. "So I figured that if there was a program that you could make that would download something in the background, so it would detect that there was something new for you and downloaded it in the background and not tell you about it, but only present the information that there was something new when it was downloaded, then your experience would be click and play."[19]

In Curry's mind, the program would function the same way as a nightly news broadcast. It would assemble all the pieces behind the scenes and present them to the viewers when they were ready to consume it.

Curry took his idea to Dave Winer, a New York software developer and entrepreneur. Winer's company, UserLand Software, had released a set of tools that allowed users to read and write RSS.

"I tried to explain to him that it would be interesting to integrate his published subscribe concept with RSS with large media objects, with large files," Curry said. "Then you could have exactly that process work where your RSS reader would detect something new and then it would to say 'Here's that something new, I've got to download that,' and then it would do that, but it wouldn't actually show up in your timeline, if you will, until it was completely downloaded."[20]

In December 2000, Winer released RSS 0.92, which, among other things, allowed audio to be aggregated via RSS feeds.[21] This was the seed from which podcasting grew. Winer released other updates to RSS, which he dubbed "Really Simple Syndication" in 2002.[22]

"And so, for a couple of years actually, we had something called Radio User-Land, which is an RSS feed builder and receiver and a blogging tool at the same time," Curry said. "You could subscribe to other blogs, and it was a nice little application."[23]

The next step in podcasting's evolution took place in 2003. Winer, who was now working at the Harvard Berkman Center, updated his RSS software to allow readers to access and subscribe to journalist Christopher Lydon's audioblog. At the time, Lydon was conducting interviews and including MP3 files with his posts. Thanks to Winer's update, listeners could now receive automatic downloads of Lydon's audio posts. Lydon would go on to create the first podcast, *Radio Open Source*, which he continues to host to this day.[24]

Podcasting had a process, a way for people to get content. With *Radio Open Source*, they now had something to download and listen to. In these early days, though, users didn't really have a way to listen to content except via their desktop computers. What they really needed was a player they could take with them.

"Around 2004, a little bit before that, I was introduced to the iPod," Curry said. "It was being sold as a jukebox really, a device for music. And I looked at it and I said, 'How can we put all the kinds of stuff you could put a radio show on here in MP3?' So we already had these RSS feeds and the receive part working, and I created a little AppleScript and it would go out and parse an RSS feed. And then if there was a new item in this RSS feed—it was a special one, which only included pretty much MP3 entries—it would look at that and say, 'OK, time to download,' and then once it was downloaded this little AppleScript would then trigger it to be loaded onto the iPod. Then, if you left that overnight and you checked it the next morning, if there'd been something new, the publisher would already be loaded onto the iPod."[25]

Curry admitted that the AppleScript was about the limit of his technical expertise. However, his experience in broadcasting would contribute to the medium's advancing even further.

"We already had the publishing side done, so the people can create essentially a receiver for the broadcast mechanism that was in place and knowing full well that software developers work best if you give them a new challenge every day," he said. "How about if I create a little radio show every single day [for] the developers, it was a lot of people blogging, people interested in what I was doing? So once you do that, then maybe you'll have a couple more of these receivers built, and it'll be tuned not towards blogs but more towards podcasts."[26]

Around that time, Curry and Winer launched *The Daily Source Code*, an audio podcast aimed at software developers.

"Source code is what developers work in all day, and it'll be daily, and they'll have something fresh and new to check out," Curry said. "This was a beautiful little loop that we created. It really caught fire halfway through 2004, moving towards 2005. People were calling me for interviews. 'What is this?' All kinds of just crazy stuff."[27]

One of the people who was listening to podcasts in those early days was Rob Walch, who'd just earned his MBA from the University of Connecticut. He had a lot of free time and was looking for something to occupy his attention.

FIGURE 0.4   Robert Walch is vice president of podcaster relations at Libsyn.

"I was traveling a lot, and I had an iPod, and podcasting started out here in September–October 2004," Walch said. "I thought I'd get some podcasts, and that made me want to do a podcast. I haven't had to worry about filling my spare time ever since."[28]

In late 2004, Walch launched *podCast 411*, which he described as "'Inside the Actor's Studio,' but for podcasting." He would interview podcasters about the craft of podcasting—a useful resource for people, like Walch, who were just trying to figure out how to create, post and distribute their podcasts. Although an electrical engineer, Walch had no real audio production experience when he started.

"Putting things together wasn't that difficult," he said. "But I had a Mac. I was a Mac guy, and I had GarageBand on there, and I bought the book 'Garage-Band: The Missing Manual' by David Pogue. I used that to figure out how to use GarageBand, and the rest of the stuff I just learned how to hand-code RSS feeds, because when I started, there were no tutorials how to podcast. There were none. So I was one of the first people to put a tutorial up on how to actually podcast, how to write an RSS feed and do those things."[29]

That was the first of many podcasting-related tutorials Walch would post online.

"At that point in time, I hosted it on my own server," he said. "I had an iPower; I still host to iPower Web. I just put my media files up there, and I knew I was going to hit my limit. I knew I was going to bring my site down if my show got popular."[30]

One of Walch's early interviews was with Sen. John Edwards (D-NC). He knew that the interview would garner a great deal of traffic, which would tax his server. So, he moved his podcast over to Libsyn. Short for "Liberated Syndication," Libsyn was launched in November 2004 as the first podcast hosting company.

"I knew of them [at Libsyn], and I had talked about them a couple of times on the show," Walch said. "I moved my shows over there, and that was in March 2005. I had the interview with Senator Edwards in April 2005, and I've been on Libsyn ever since."[31]

Walch joined the company in 2007 and is now vice president of podcaster relations.

"It's almost like saying it was bear skins and flint knives," Walch said. "[In] the early days, if you wanted to listen to a podcast, it was almost as difficult as making a podcast. You had to go get a third-party program called iPodderX [www.wired.com/2004/10/ipodderx_speaks/] and then you had to download that. Then you had to sync from that to iTunes, and from iTunes you had to sync to your iPod. . . . I scratch my head and think, 'Why the heck did I jump into it so much at that time?' because iTunes wasn't supporting it yet. But you could see the potential for it."[32]

In June 2005, Apple released iTunes version 4.9, which added podcast support and removed many of the remaining barriers to listenership.

"And then two years later, when the iPhone came out, that's really where the biggest challenge was overcome, and that was by putting this multimedia device that could get consumption on the go in your hand," Walch said. "Those were the two biggest inflection points in podcasts: iTunes and the launch of the iPhone."[33]

Today, 75 percent of all downloads are direct to mobile devices.[34]

"Back then, in 2005, it was none, essentially," Walch said. "That's how much things have changed. That makes life a lot different for consumption for the end user. They can get their podcasts whenever they want it. They can play Angry Birds; they can listen to a podcast. Podcasting has become that simple to consume. The podcast hub for consumption is the smartphone, and that's the way it's going to remain for a long, long time."[35]

Walch's second podcast, which started as *Today in iPhone* and is now known as *Today in iOS*, was launched in April 2007 as an excuse for Walch to buy himself an iPhone.

"It was the first podcast about the iPhone," Walch said. "I launched it before the iPhone launched. It's been very successful, and I've been writing about iOS products since. I've got a whole bunch of them."

In 2004, Todd Cochrane, host of *Geek News Central* and co-host of *The New Media Show* podcasts, was active-duty in the U.S. Navy, "flying a desk" after being injured overseas, when podcasting entered his life.

"I was looking for any opportunity to make myself useful, and I ended up in Waco, Texas, doing contractor support for the Navy, babysitting aircraft that were going through modifications," he said. "Because I was still wearing a clamshell from a broken back, one of those body-cast-type things, I was spending a lot of time indoors because it was doggone hot in Texas. I was a fan of Dave Winer already and what he was doing over at scripting. com; when he started doing the *Daily Source Code* with Adam Curry, it lit a fire."[36]

Already an active blogger, Cochrane, who is now the president and CEO of Raw Voice (the parent company of the Blubrry podcasting hosting service), began recording podcasts out of his Texas hotel room.

"The podcast went from zero listeners to about 45,000 listeners in the first 90 days," he said. "Back then, there was no unlimited hosting like we offer with our company, so it was a purely a matter of just trying to keep the show online with the audience growth. It was pretty incredible."[37]

In December 2004, Cochrane received an email from Wiley Publishing asking him to write the first book on podcasting. The resulting "Podcasting: Do-It-Yourself Guide" was published in May 2005 and went on to sell more than 40,000 copies. "The fateful thing in the podcasting space for me was that in July 2005, I got a call from GoDaddy asking to sponsor my show," he said. "What that led to was them wanting to basically advertise in more podcasts. I figured out that there was a business there, and that's where Raw Voice came from, from a conversation with a GoDaddy rep wanting to advertise in more shows. That old saying, 'You'd rather have 1 percent of 100 people's money or 100 percent of your own'? Well, I understood the value in having a little piece of everything. We really jumped into advertising big in 2005, and the show continued to grow as well."[38]

Raw Voice eventually started several different websites, but the Blubrry podcast hosting platform became the flagship site that the company's business revolves around today. It is the second-largest platform (after Libsyn).

Currently, Blubrry has almost 300,000 podcasts. That's the full directory, though not all of those podcasts are hosted by the company.

"We've publicly stated that we have over 40,000 customers using our statistics platforms," Cochrane said. "We also have companies—like ESPN, ABC, Moody Radio—that use our enterprise podcast statistics platform, which is a separate product from what normal podcasters get, similar but a little more deeper dive."[39]

He added that a large number of podcasts hosting on Blubrry do so to take advantage of PowerPress, the company's audio-player plugin for WordPress.

Much as for Walch, Cochrane's early enthusiasm, his faith in the power of podcasting, and his hard work led to bigger things. Out of nothing, sitting in a hotel room, he began to build a business.

"My first day of recording a show was quite rudimentary," Cochrane said. "I went to Walmart and picked up a Labtec headset and recorded my first seven episodes on a $14.95 headset. Those were great, fun days, but now I have a studio that's pretty incredible. I started from very humble beginnings."[40]

Potential podcasters should take inspiration from stories like these and the others contained in this book, but they also need to be aware of the realities of the podcasting environment.

"A lot of these articles want you to think that there is something holding podcasting back from a hockey-stick growth," Walch said. "There will never be a hockey-stick growth. The hockey-stick growth happened in 2005 when Apple launched iTunes support. Ever since then, it's been steady growth, and smartphones helped accelerate that growth. Podcasting is long-form content. It's not 140 characters. It's not viral. It's not a Grumpy Cat. It's not a video of a kid getting hit in the crotch with a skateboard. It's not that. Podcasting is a long form. It's a longer play. There is no hockey-stick growth ever coming to this medium, but there is growth coming, and there's been growth consistently going along. There was never a down time. There was never a resurgence in podcasting. There was a resurgence of podcast coverage by media, but podcast consumption—there was never a down point to it. It's consistently grown, quarter over quarter, year over year."[41]

Looking at the listenership data from Edison Research and seeing the large number of downloads *Serial* garnered, it's easy to come away with the impression that podcast success is just a few easy steps away. It's not.

In September 2013, an average podcast episode was downloaded 141 times 30 days after it had been made live, according to Walch. Episodes with 3,400 downloads after a month were in the top 10 percent of all podcasts, while 9,000 downloads put you in the top 5 percent. Big shows, the ones that routinely appear at the top of iTunes ratings, are in the elite 1 percent of podcasts being produced.[42]

"If your whole idea of getting into podcasting is to get a podcast and monetize that podcast, you have about a 1 percent chance of doing that," Walch said. "The big difference between podcasting and becoming an actor is you don't have to move to L.A. and become a waiter to support your craft. You can stay where you are. Some podcasts are going to do huge, and they're going to make money, and you're going to have people who are celebrities in one field coming over into the other field and becoming a celebrity in podcasting, like Tim Ferriss (*The Tim Ferriss Show*, http://fourhourworkweek.com/podcast/), who had a built-in audience, or Joe Rogan (*The Joe Rogan Experience*, http://podcasts.joerogan.net), who had a built-in audience."[43]

Comedian Marc Maron, whose *WTF* podcast (www.wtfpod.com) consistently places at the top of the iTunes charts, started podcasting after his radio career at Air America fizzled.

"His comedy career, he'll tell you, was over at that point," Walch said. "Air America folded, and he decided to do the podcast rather than suicide. It was one last go. And Marc took off, and the show is great. And now he can go anywhere in the country and sell out venues for comedy, but he built that up from nothing. But he had a good background and a good comedic background and contacts, and that helped him. But it wasn't that he came in with celebrity. So there's been people like that. And Dan Carlin (host of *Hardcore History*, www.dancarlin.com). Nobody knew who Dan Carlin was before he started his podcast. Now he's one of the three biggest podcasts out there, 4 million downloads an episode."[44]

The podcasts that will rise quickly to the top and that many networks—like PodcastOne—are betting on are ones with large, pre-existing audiences or celebrity recognition.

But if those types of podcasts account for only 1 percent of all podcasts being produced, who is making the remaining 99 percent?

Well, I'm one of them. *It's All Journalism* is aimed at digital journalists, a very niche audience. Most of the podcasters I interviewed for this book are podcasting because they love what they're doing and find rewards in many things besides audience size. Some are monetizing their podcasts, but many aren't.

One of the things you need to understand before you begin podcasting is that your potential audience may not be that large. Remember what Walch said: The average podcast episode receives 141 downloads after 30 days.

"If you're doing a podcast on the Kansas City startup scene, you're never going to get above 1,000 listeners to your podcast," he said. "Set your level of expectation correctly. If you're doing a podcast on professional pig raising—there is a podcast like that, the *Swinecast* (www.swinecast.com)—understand that your audience is going to be very small. You're not looking at 100,000 downloads. You're looking at 500 or 200 downloads for a professional pig-raising podcast, you've hit a grand slam. You've hit every professional pig raiser in the United States."[45]

What podcasting gives you is a level playing field to get your voice out there. You don't need to go through a network. You don't need to ask anyone's permission. You don't need to spend thousands of dollars on recording equipment and a fancy studio. It's just you, your microphone, a recorder and your audience. You may be talking to 141 people or 1 million. They're your audience, and they want to hear what you have to say.

Let's get started.

NOTES

1 The Podcast Consumer 2016, Edison Research (2016, June). [www.edisonresearch. com/wp-content/uploads/2016/05/The-Podcast-Consumer-2016.pdf]
2 Webster, Tom (2016, June 20). Phone interview.
3 Ibid.
4 Ibid.
5 Quirk, Vanessa, "Guide to podcasting, Tow Center for Digital Journalism," Columbia University (2015, Dec.). [http://towcenter.org/research/guide-to-podcasting/]
6 Hesse, Monica, " 'Serial' takes the stand: How a podcast became a character in its own narrative," *The Washington Post* (2016, Feb. 8). [www.washingtonpost. com/lifestyle/when-a-post-conviction-hearing-feels-like-a-sequel-the-weird ness-of-serial-back-on-the-stand/2016/02/08/b3782c60-2a49-48f7-9480-a34d-d9e07ab6_story.html]
7 "Serial/This American Life/Chicago Public Media," 74th Annual Peabody award winners (2015, May 31). [www.peabodyawards.com/award-profile/serial]
8 Webster.
9 Ibid.
10 Friedman, Lex, "Apple: One billion iTunes podcast subscriptions and counting," *Macworld* (2013, July 22). [www.macworld.com/article/2044958/apple-one-billion-itunes-podcast-subscriptions-and-counting.html]
11 Webster.
12 Pattiz, Norman (2016, June 14). Phone interview.
13 Ibid.
14 Ibid.
15 Monaghan, Brendan (2016, June 14). Phone interview.

16 "Guglielmo Marconi" (1896, June 2). *Wikipedia*. [https://en.wikipedia.org/wiki/ Guglielmo_Marconi]

17 "RSS" (2000, Dec. 8). *Wikipedia*. [https://en.wikipedia.org/wiki/RSS]

18 Curry, Adam (2016, Aug. 16). Phone interview.

19 Ibid.

20 Ibid.

21 Winer, Dave (2000, Dec. 25). "RSS 0.92 specification," UserLand Software. Retrieved Oct. 31, 2006.

22 "RSS."

23 Curry.

24 Quirk.

25 Curry.

26 Ibid.

27 Ibid.

28 Walch, Robert (2016, May 23). Phone interview.

29 Ibid.

30 Ibid.

31 Ibid.

32 Ibid.

33 Ibid.

34 Ibid.

35 Ibid.

36 Cochrane, Todd (2016, May 23). Phone interview.

37 Ibid.

38 Ibid.

39 Ibid.

40 Ibid.

41 Walch.

42 Ibid.

43 Ibid.

44 Ibid.

45 Ibid.

1

The Tenets of Good Podcasting

The first and most important thing you need to ask yourself is "Should I be doing a podcast?"

If you're reading a book about how to do podcasts, you probably have an answer already. Or at least you think you do.

This is the moment to face some hard truths about podcasting.

As stated in the introduction, unless you're a famous wrestler, reality star or celebrity, you're going to start off with a small audience. You can grow that audience over time with a lot of hard work, but your audience is going to be smaller than you think—a lot smaller.

You need to have a passion for your topic.

Nearly all the podcasters interviewed for this book stressed the importance of having a passion for your topic, almost above any other piece of advice they had to offer. For this reason, it's the first tenet of podcasting: Have a passion for the topic. Are you going to be as excited about this topic in episode 200 as you were in episode 1?

If the topic doesn't make, and keep, you fired up, how can you make your audience care? How can you keep them interested in what you have to say?

Adam Sachs, the former CEO of Midroll Media, said that podcasters should really love the medium and love whatever it is that they're talking about.

"I think a unique kind of a corollary similar to that is having a unique point of view and format," he said. "You know, if there are 400,000 or 500,000 podcasts out there, why are people going to choose yours? We always talk about how we're competing for people's time almost more than anything, right? There's only so many podcasts that people can listen to when you think about their daily lives and the other media that they're consuming. Coming to the table with something unique—that makes it very clear that there's a reason for people to tune in and listen. I think it is really important."[1]

Laura Mayer, director of production at Panoply, launched her first podcast early in her career.

Starting a podcast is "what made me realize what I ultimately wanted to do with my life, which ended up being making podcasts," she said. "But I think that it's a good way to kind of put yourself on the line in terms of making your voice heard in particular. And that's something that can help clarify a lot of direction for people. . . . Pick one thing you really want to talk about and you think you can talk about every week and with other people, ideally, or . . . by yourself and just try it."[2]

Despite all the hoopla around the podcasting boom, audience size should not be something that holds you back from starting a podcast.

"If the first podcast you put out there has three listeners, that's fine," Mayer said. "And it shouldn't be about listenership necessarily. There's a lot right now, of course, with the podcast boom and a lot of business interest in that kind of thing. No one, when they're starting a podcast, should necessarily think, 'I'm going to start my first podcast and I'm going to be a star.' I think that starting your first podcast is a great way to find your own voice and . . . figure out how you can best utilize it in whatever medium you end up making things in."[3]

PODCASTING IS HARD; DO THE WORK

Producing a podcast with any regularity is difficult. Beyond having passion for the topic, you need to be committed to doing the work necessary to succeed.

"It's hard," said Todd Cochrane, CEO of Raw Voice, the company behind the Blubrry podcast hosting platform. "This is hard. I always tell content creators that ask me this question, 'Are you passionate enough to talk a couple times a week about a topic for two years? Is there enough stuff in your head, or is there enough material or enough people, to be able to sustain a show for a couple of years?' "[4]

Two years is not just a magic number Cochrane pulled out of the air.

"I'd like them to think about two years instead of six weeks or seven weeks, because what we see—and this number has stayed pretty steady throughout the years—about 50 percent of shows, new shows, never make it to episode 7," he said. "They quit. They figure, 'Oh, I've only got 100 people listening to me' or 'I only got 50, and I'm doing horrible and this is too hard.' If they can make it past [episode] 7, usually those shows that do, they'll make it to about episode 25. That's where we see another drop-off. We typically will lose some more there.

"Doing audio content, while it seems easy, you have to have fresh stuff to talk about. If you don't have a topic that lends itself to feeding you fresh information every week, you're going to have a very, very tough time."[5]

You need a constant flow of fresh ideas, a good topic, enthusiasm for that topic and the energy to keep a podcast going week in and week out for an indefinite period of time.

"For me, it's easy. I do a tech show," said Cochrane, who hosts *Geek News Central* and co-hosts *The New Media Show*. "There's always new stuff. But if I was doing a show talking to business leaders, then I'd have to be scrambling every week to get a guest or two booked to get them interviewed. That's hard, hard work. For me, I do an hour-and-a-half, two hours' worth of research, and, bam, I'm up and running. I do a 70-minute show and it just flows. But [for] some of these other folks, it can be a real struggle."[6]

A typical 35-minute episode of *It's All Journalism*, for example, takes about 45 minutes to an hour to record. But before we even turn on the microphones, hours of work go into pre-production, from choosing and researching a topic, to finding a guest or guests, to juggling schedules, to determining whether we're going to record in studio or by phone or Skype and writing up questions. That's all the work *before* the interview. Once the audio is in the can, it's post-production time. We have to edit it, upload it to our audio server, write up a story to accompany the audio on our website and share it out on social media. It's almost a second job.

"The biggest advice is 'Understand that it's going to be hard and, if you're going to talk about something, you have to have a topic you're super passionate about,'" Cochrane said.[7]

Fresh out of college, Megan Tan, creator of Radiotopia's *Millennial* podcast, faced a lot of uncertainty and insecurity about producing her first podcast episode. Although she had a degree in photojournalism, what she really wanted to do was audio storytelling for radio, but she had no experience and no idea how to start out.

"*Millennial* was not supposed to be like a sustainable podcast," she said. "It was not to have been for a whole bunch of strangers to hear, really. It was just like a portfolio piece. I essentially wanted to become a radio producer. I didn't know where to begin. So I thought, 'Why not make a portfolio that I can show future employers?' And that was *Millennial*."[8]

The first season of *Millennial* follows Tan as she moves out of her parents' home and into her boyfriend's apartment, finds a part-time job as a waitress and—with a great deal of trepidation—launches her podcast.

"Nothing was really planned, to be honest," Tan said. "I really felt like I didn't have the confidence to go out and essentially talk to people and tell them

FIGURE 1.1   Megan Tan is the host of *Millennial*.

I was a reporter or a producer, because in my mind I wasn't one yet. I just thought: 'Why not pull from an experience that's right under my feet? I've analyzed and read a lot of books about story and narrative. And I know what makes a really great narrative. Story is change.' And I thought, 'Man, in your 20s, all you do is change.'"[9]

A PODCAST IS A PROMISE; POST REGULAR EPISODES ON TIME

One of the key decisions you need to make when you're planning a podcast is how often you expect to post a new episode. Will it be monthly, bimonthly, weekly, biweekly, daily? It's important for a couple of reasons.

First, determining how often episodes are posted will help establish the workflow. Be realistic about how much time you have to commit. If you're doing it as a hobby or a once-in-a-while thing, posting biweekly or monthly is probably an easy stretch.

The downside of taking so long to post, though, is it's harder to build an audience when there's too much time between episodes.

FIGURE 1.2 John Lee Dumas is the host of *EOFire*.

John Lee Dumas posts a new episode of his podcast *EOFire* (*Entrepreneur on Fire*) seven days a week.

"Back in 2012, I was, every day, driving to a job I did not like at all, and kind of my solace was to listen to audio books," he said. "That got a little expensive, because audio books aren't cheap. So, I kind of found podcasts as a great, free, targeted, and just valuable source of the audio for my commutes to work and workouts at the gym."[10]

Dumas gobbled up all the entrepreneur-based podcasts he could find, like *Planet Money, Freakomonics* and Pat Flynn's *Smart Passive Income Podcast.*

"I was like, these guys have got something going," Dumas said. "It's pretty cool. But the problem is Pat's only doing two a month. I need more content than that. I'm driving to work five days a week. I'm hitting the gym three or four days a week. So I said, 'I need to find a daily podcast that's interviewing entrepreneurs so that I can have one every single day as I'm driving to work.' It didn't exist. And I said: 'You know what? I don't like my job and I love Gandhi.' And he says, 'Be the change you want to see in the world.' I wanted to see a seven-day-a-week podcast exist—it didn't. I said: 'Why not me? Let's do this.'"[11]

On the other end of the spectrum, you have someone like Dan Carlin, who releases a new episode of *Hardcore History* every three or four months. Those episodes, however, are highly researched and detailed, professionally produced audio performances—lectures, almost—about significant moments in history. They're gems of long-form storytelling, well worth the wait.

Likewise, there are episodic podcasts like *Serial* that run season-to-season, almost a throwback to network television days when people waited over the summer for the new season of their favorite show. It's the level of quality found in *Serial* and *Hardcore History* that make them different. The audience is willing to wait a little longer for something special.

"The ones I've seen be really, really successful are folks that [aren't] just punching a clock, but they're doing something they're passionate about," said Brendan Monaghan, CEO of Panoply. "They're engaging thoroughly with their audience, and they're doing everything they can to build that growth and all the other stuff. All of this stuff comes once you kind of find your stride and you're consistent. That's the other thing worth mentioning;

that consistency is huge. If you're just doing this every other week or every third week, people can't rely on you."[12]

Panoply is a network of podcasts, including those produced by *Slate* magazine. He tells the story of one time when the *Slate* staff was late in posting a weekly episode of the *Political Gabfest* podcast.

One of the show's hosts, David Plotz, received an angry call from a listener asking why the podcast hadn't been posted. Plotz explained that technical difficulties had prevented them from completing the episode on time.

Monaghan continued: "He was like, 'Well, I host a television program and every Friday I listen to you guys so I can be educated on my show.' [Plotz] said: 'Well, you might. If you don't mind me asking, sir, may I ask you what show you host?' and he's like: 'Yeah, this is Stephen Colbert and I host "The Colbert Report." And I come to listen to your show every Friday.'

"It is a funny anecdote but a true indication of how people come to rely on that consistency of production," Monaghan said.[13]

Podcasting is a promise you make to your audience. If you say you're going to post every Friday morning, you'd better post every Friday morning, or your audience will find something else to listen to.

START SHORTER; EARN LONGER

Podcasters like to debate what the ideal length of an episode should be. Some episodes can be a few minutes, whereas others can go on for hours.

When we started *It's All Journalism*, a typical episode was around 50 minutes, and sometimes we went over an hour. We did very little editing, and the content was conversational. It meandered all over the place. Now our episodes come in around 30 to 35 minutes. We edit a bit more and keep the conversations tight.

Hosts Ernesto Gluecksmann and Blake Althen launched their business-themed *Through the Noise* podcast as a way to have entertaining conversations with CEOs and entrepreneurs.

"We aim for about 20 minutes, but we don't cut off anybody," Gluecksmann said. "If they're on a good story or a rant or roll, we'll let it go. But, about an hour is the max for us. But I think with some guests, I could just keep going on and do a three-hour podcast. With some guests, 20 minutes can be a long time, so it just depends on who you have and the feel you have with the person."[14]

According to Gluecksmann, the podcast is lightly edited, which helps maintain its "dinner conversation" feel.

"I was pretty adamant with Blake that I didn't want us to sound too polished in any way," he said. "I want more of a real conversation. That might be different, I think, with some of the other podcasts that are out there. That makes it real to me. That makes it feel like there are two people in a genuine conversation. It's not something that's been scripted. It's not something that you're trying to get the right sound bite at the right time. If you're going to ask listeners to give an hour of their time, it should be as honest of a conversation as you can possibly have. That's just our style of the show. There are other shows that do really well scripting and carefully editing and all that kind of stuff as well."[15]

Mayer spent five and a half years doing audio production at WNYC, a public radio station in New York City, before joining Panoply as a producer. In her new job, she spent five days a week editing Panoply's many podcasts.

"At the time, I didn't really know what I was getting myself into," she said. "For the first six months, it was just me and one other producer, who started as a freelancer, and we ended up hiring, producing all the podcasts that we produce in house, which was a lot of editing, a lot of production. In addition to the two of us, we had this sort of fleet of freelancers that are based in New York and then other places in the country—I called it the Wizard of Oz school of podcast production—where they would be on the line listening to the podcast, producing it from afar and then editing it. So we had producers, editors and then an engineer in the studio actually running the recording or me and the producer in the studio, who's not an engineer, just making sure the recording happened."[16]

In her current role as production manager, Mayer isn't quite as hands-on as she once was, but she oversees Panoply's podcasts. All this experience gives her a unique perspective on the ideal length of a podcast episode.

"We don't have a specific number," she said. "But our idea is you start shorter, you earn longer. So our suggestion to people who are starting a podcast is

'Think very, very, very carefully about what kind of conversation you want to have or what kind of topics you want to do.' And try it out. If you're getting to listeners or even if you're getting the listener interaction that you're looking for, maybe they want more. Maybe people will get in touch with you and say 'I want longer; I want to cover this; I want you to cover that.' Our sort of motto's 'Start shorter,' meaning a half an hour. 'Earn longer,' meaning an hour-plus."[17]

EVERY EPISODE IS AN AUDITION

Another important guideline that may seem obvious but people tend to forget about is to produce quality content that people will enjoy listening and coming back to again and again.

"Being entertaining and informative is critical," said former Midroll CEO Sachs. "I think people often forget that it should be entertaining. You should want to listen to it and be delighted by listening to this podcast. I think a little more on the logistics side, having regular consistent releases is really important to building an audience, and building that expectation of 'It's Thursday morning; when I open Stitcher, when I bring my Overcast (or whatever app you use like that), my new episode is going to be waiting there for me,' I think, is really important."[18]

Likewise, make sure your audio sounds good. "Some people are more tolerant than others of poor audio quality, but for the most part, it can really damage a listener's enjoyment if the show does sound like crap," Sachs said.[19]

Nick DePrey is the innovation accountant and analytics manager for NPR One, the public radio corporation's streaming news and podcast app. What that fancy job title means is that he's basically a scorekeeper.

"Everything we do with NPR One for the last two years has been largely experimental," he said. "We're always trying to learn from what we're doing. My job is to conclude the results of those experiments and help us do better next time. One of the things that we realized with NPR One is it's not just an experimental product, but it is a way to analyze the actual performance. Relative performance shows episodes in ways that, to my knowledge, we've never been able to do in the industry before."[20]

DePrey and the people he works with study listener data—things like how long people listen, what shows are their favorites and at what point they typically bail out of an episode—collected by the NPR One player app. They're able to draw conclusions from their observations and make recommendations to producers on how to adjust the content of a podcast to improve performance.

One significant piece of information DePrey discovered is a general pattern of how long a user will give an episode before he or she decides to listen to something else.

"The battle is won or lost in the first two minutes. . . . There's not something that you can do in minutes 10 to 20 to make up for an intro that didn't hold the audience's attention," he said. "If you are not justifying why the audience is with you in the first two minutes, you will lose them. . . . This is something that maybe we thought we knew, but now we're hopefully seeing it for the first time. Every piece is an audition."[21]

Hook your audience early and keep them engaged with intriguing, unique content in every single episode. Never phone it in. This week's episode may be your 200th, but it's also the first time somebody has ever heard your show.

As DePrey said, "Every piece is an audition."

There are enough barriers already to creating a successful podcast; don't give people a reason to skip out on you. It's hard to win them back.

Israeli podcaster Ran Levi launched *Curious Minds* as a way to expose other "curious minds" to heady topics like history, philosophy, economics and quantum mechanics. His specialty is taking complex ideas and making them understandable to audiences who may have grown up thinking science and technology are boring.

One of the tactics Levi uses to keep his audience coming back is to not tell them what the next episode is going to be about.

"I know that if I'm going to say to the audience, the next episode will be about, for example, a subject in mathematics, there will be many people who would probably say to themselves: 'Oh, math—it must be so boring. Let's just skip the next episode,'" he said. "I try to surprise them. By the time they understand the episode is about mathematics, it's already too late. They downloaded it. They have no chance. Now they have to hear me. And then they understand that, yes, math can be interesting. Physics can be amazing. Just be open to new ideas."[22]

FIGURE 1.3   Ran Levi hosts the *Curious Minds* podcast.

What unique perspective can you add to the conversation?

Successful podcasting is more than just turning on a microphone and talking. You have to have something interesting to say, and it has to be different from the 500,000 other podcasts that are already out there.

Caitlin Thompson, director of U.S. content for the Swedish-based podcasting network Acast, believes that a successful podcast has three components.

"You don't have to have all of them, but you have to have at least one or two of them," she said. "Number one, you have to have a really strong host. A strong host can make up for a lot of shortcomings. You don't have to have a strong host. An example I'll give of a show without a strong host is *Modern Love*. It's a great show. It's super interesting. It's not hosted, because it doesn't need to be. It's a storytelling show."[23]

Modern Love is based on the long-running New York Times feature about relationships in the modern world. Each episode revolves around one of the previously published non-fiction Times essays. An actor reads the essay, the Times editor offers his take on what inspired him to publish the piece and the author discusses how his or her life has changed since it was published.

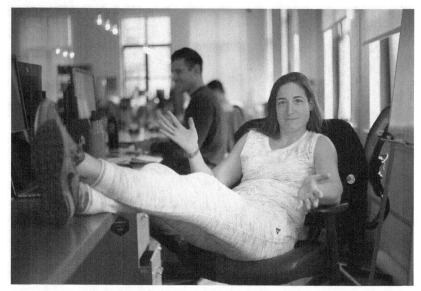

FIGURE 1.4 Caitlin Thompson is the director of U.S. content for the Acast podcasting network.

"But having a host who is compelling and captivating and can be an audience proxy," Thompson said, "because they're curious and they're interested or they're there like a tour guide to their little world, is really useful."[24]

Even without a good host, or no host at all, a podcast can succeed if its format is really strong, which is Thompson's second must-have. She pointed to *Song Exploder* as an example of a format-driven podcast.

"It's got an incredibly broad topic, which is to say songs—songs of any type, of any genre, about anything really," she said. "But the format is bulletproof. It's 14 minutes, give or take a minute. It's a song. You hear the story of how it got made. You hear snippets of it, and the end always culminates in you hearing the entire song. It's one of the most satisfying audio experiences I can imagine, and it's very simple. And the host, Hrishikesh Hirway, is in it for maybe 10 seconds, just to literally introduce what song it is this week, and the rest of it is voices of the creators. Again, that show is all format. It's also minimal topic, minimal host."[25]

Thompson's third element for a successful podcast is having a strong topic.

"There are a lot of shows that are really, really, really broad, and I would argue that's another mistake people make, which is like, 'Oh, I'm an interesting enough person; I can just have a really broad show.' Really? Are you the most interesting person that you know? If so, you don't know that many people. But you can make up for it by being like: 'I am a fairly interesting person, but I have an incredibly deep obsessive hobby of making balsa wood airplanes. And I can podcast for everybody who wants to know about balsa wood airplanes—it [this audience] might be small, but there are people who are going to want to do my show. Nay, they're going to have to listen to my show, because I'm one of the only people in the world who knows how to talk about this in a way that's compelling.'"[26]

Many people who never had access to the mainstream media before are finally having their voices and perspectives heard through podcasts.

Sarah van Mosel, chief commercial officer at Acast, works with Thompson to grow their network's audience. Often that means bringing in diverse voices and content.

"She and I actually worked together at WNYC before we came here," van Mosel said. "Her mission was to say: 'Hey, what if we didn't just go after the usual suspects or just like white men and comedy or the public media? Or we courted, you know, women of color, [the] LGBT community. What if we get brown people? What if we did that? What would happen?'"[27]

When they began bringing more diverse hosts into the fold, huge new audiences came with them.

"If you look at the Edison media research about women listening to podcasts, it's doubled since 2013," van Mosel said. "And guess what? So has the number of women that are hosting podcasts. They're bringing new audiences with them. There's that whole idea of like, 'Hey, you know, go where the usual suspects aren't.' The same sort of philosophy behind sharing your episode on Twitter, where people who might not be podcast listeners will see it and have access to it. Then they'll become podcast listeners because you're engaging them with amazing content. Same idea with the kind of shows. You're bringing in new audiences and making the whole pie even bigger."[28]

One of Acast's podcasts is the syndicated *FuseBox Radio Broadcast*, which Mary Nichols founded in 1998, years before podcasts even existed. She and

FIGURE 1.5 Mary Nichols, host of *FuseBox Radio Broadcast*, was podcasting before there was podcasting.

co-host Jon Pac record the weekly mix of commentary and music in Washington, DC.

"I think our thing is we always promote ourselves as being like average black people in America," Nichols said. "We'll talk about these topics in terms of politics and stuff. Sometimes we'll also talk about, 'Hey, how do you feel about the latest X-Men movie?' And, you know, other stuff in between, because we have multiple, diverse interests."[29]

She continued: "I think one of the things that's lacking for multiple lines of conversation for everybody in our mainstream media culture is that you don't really get to see a diverse persona . . . you'll go to let's say Fox News, and the first thing people be like is Republican. That's it. You'll go to another news channel, they'll be like only promoting this country or they only talk about this particular type of music."[30]

Podcasting is giving audiences access to authentic voices with which they can identify.

"I think we have a new media audience that's, in a sad way, almost used to people just being fake," Nichols said. "Or being stuck in a particular box in terms of what they can talk about. They're going to a podcast to hear part of a real person. And ultimately, I think that's the best thing."[31]

IMAGINE THE PERSON YOU'RE TALKING TO

Ultimately, the reason you're creating a podcast is so people will listen. Identifying your audience before you start recording will make it easier for you to create content they can relate to and find enjoyable.

Therefore, it's important to determine whether the audience you're trying to reach actually listens to podcasts. Although Edison Research shows that awareness of podcasting is growing, about three-quarters of Americans aren't regular podcast listeners.

It will be difficult enough trying to convince people to listen to your particular podcast. Don't make trying to convert people to podcasting your primary battle. Your focus should be on promoting your content to people who are already podcast listeners. Let the networks, like Acast, Panoply and Midroll, work on growing the pie.

When we started *It's All Journalism*, I imagined the typical audience member would be someone like me—a middle-aged journalist, looking for information about digital technology and new ways of storytelling.

We discovered pretty quickly that our core audience skewed much younger. They were fresh out of college, seeking full-time media jobs or working as unpaid interns, trying to learn skills that they hadn't been taught in J-school. They were millennials, early adopters of digital technology who were used to listening to audio content on their smartphones. In other words, they listened to podcasts.

That middle-aged journalist struggling to figure out how to cover a big story using Twitter had no time for or interest in us. We pivoted our focus to serve that new audience.

It also helps to put some thought into what you're going to call your podcast, to make it easy for your audience to identify what it's about.

When David Jackson, founder of *The School of Podcasting*, first launched the podcast for his school, he called it *The Morning Announcements*.

"Get it? Because it's *The School of Podcasting*," Jackson said. "But if I went up to somebody and said, 'Hey, I'm doing a show called *The Morning Announcements*—what do you think it's about?' they'd probably say, 'Well, maybe it's a podcast for principals or school or something like that.' Nobody would ever guess podcasting. You want your show's name to be obvious."[32]

Another time, one of Jackson's clients wanted to name his podcast *After the Darkness*.

"I said, 'Go find your target audience,'" Jackson said. "That's the key point: Find your target audience and say: 'I'm going to do a show called *After the Darkness*. What do you think it's about?' So he did, and somebody said, 'Isn't that a vampire movie?' Somebody else thought it was a band from the '90s."[33]

No one the client asked could guess what the subject of the podcast was, so Jackson asked him what the show was about.

"And he goes, 'Oh, it's about my life after blindness,'" Jackson said. "And I go: 'That's the name of your show. Go back to your target audience; say, "I'm going to do a show called *Life After Blindness*. What do you think it's about?"' All of them said, 'your life after blindness.'"

As this anecdote makes clear, giving your show too vague a name can make it harder for you to reach your intended audience. On the other end of the spectrum, some people feel compelled to come up with a name that has a clever double meaning. Jackson advised that it's not worth the effort: "Your show's title is kind of a headline, and I see people just waste valuable time. They go inside baseball and, for lack of a better phrase, go where there is some sort of inside joke."[34]

So your best choice is to keep the name specific and straightforward. Tan, creator of *Millennial*, has the advantage of having a podcast whose title is the audience she is trying to reach.

"*Millennial* is called *Millennial* because it's for millennials," she said. "The audience is so specific, and it's about a millennial going through their 20s. I think having a niche audience really helps turn it into a podcast that can be sustainable."[35]

She sees her podcast as a conversation between two close friends.

"With *Millennial*, because it's all about my life, you get to know intimately one person over time and, because all of this is happening in real time, you feel like you're growing with that person as they grow," she said. "I feel like radio and audio is already so intimate that when you add those extra characteristics that come with the show, it becomes even more intimate. You really squeeze the juice out of this medium, and that's what I love about audio: the intimacy."[36]

To maintain that intimate feel, Tan employs a simple strategy.

"Every single time I make an episode, I'm speaking to the same friend, right?" she said. "I'm speaking to two people intimately. As you have, essentially, one person symbolize who your audience is, you actually capture a wider net and the people you're really reaching. I feel like when I make *Millennial* and I make it for two people, that's why it's able to touch thousands. Because people feel like I'm personally talking to them, even if I'm not."[37]

Dumas, host of the *EOFire* podcast, takes that strategy one step further. Every time he does a podcast, he imagines he's talking to an imaginary audience member named "Jimmy."

"He's 36 years old," Dumas said. "He has a wife and two kids, ages 3 and 5. He has a 25-minute commute to work to a cubicle that he doesn't like for nine hours and then he drives home. He gets stuck in traffic, so he has a 32-minute commute home, cause it's a little longer because of the traffic. Gets home. Hangs out with his kids. Has dinner with his family. Puts his kids to bed. He hangs out with his wife. Then he sits on the couch and he says, 'Why do I spend 90 percent of my waking hours doing what I don't want to do?' Jimmy—I could go on for another 20 minutes about him—should be listening to *EOFire* every morning as he drives to work and every afternoon as he drives home, because that's that show that's going to inspire him."[38]

Dumas recommends that every podcaster imagine an avatar, someone who represents their audience, and speak directly to that person.

"What makes a good podcast is somebody actually knows that one listener inside and out, like I know Jimmy, and speaks to that person throughout the podcast," he said. "The other thing that makes a good podcast is stories. People resonate with stories. That's why you hear me talk about my podcast—I'll say: 'Take me to the moment in time. Was it raining? Was it dark out?' I want the person to bring us to that moment and tell us that story, because we resonate with stories as human beings, and that's really important. That's a powerful thing. The stories are huge. Knowing your avatar is really huge. And just always coming from a place of value, saying how I added value to my listeners. Always have that at the forethought of everything you do."[39]

When you decide to create a podcast, it should be a value-plus proposition for your audience. Connect with them. Figure out who they are. Establish a routine for when you're going to post a new episode so that they can check in with you regularly, like a best friend would.

And like a friend, you'll want to work hard to create unique content that will stimulate and entertain them and also make them want to share that content with others.

A podcast is not just you talking into a microphone. It's you having a conversation with your audience. Make it a good one.

ACTIVITIES

1. What makes your podcast special? One of the hardest things about podcasting is coming up with a topic that you feel passionate about and that is different enough from other podcasts already out there. Pick a topic for your podcast and then listen to episodes of three other podcasts that cover a similar topic. Write out what they have in common (e.g., how often they post, how many hosts they have, number of segments) and what they each do differently. Next, write down how your podcast will be different from the ones you listened to.

2. What's in a name? Choose 10 names for your podcast, and pick your three favorites. Ask five people which of those three names they like best. Ask them what they think your podcast is about based on that name. If they don't identify your topic, ask them whether the other two names are better now that they know what your podcast is about.

3. Try to imagine who your target audience is. In fact, take a page from John Lee Dumas of *EOFire* and create a profile of your own "Jimmy." Write a short biography of your target listener, giving him or her a name and filling in all his or her personal history. Then, write this person an email explaining why he or she should listen to your podcast. Be sure to go into detail why your podcast is the perfect one for this person to listen to.

NOTES

1 Sachs, Adam (2016, Aug. 18). Phone interview.
2 Mayer, Laura (2016, June 8). Phone interview.
3 Ibid.
4 Cochrane, Todd (2016, May 23). Phone interview.
5 Ibid.
6 Ibid.
7 Ibid.
8 Tan, Megan (2016, Aug. 4). Phone interview.
9 Ibid.
10 Dumas, John Lee (2016, July 14). Skype interview.
11 Ibid.
12 Monaghan, Brendan (2016, June 14). Phone interview.
13 Ibid.
14 Gluecksmann, Ernesto (2016, May 6). Personal interview.
15 Ibid.
16 Mayer.
17 Ibid.
18 Sachs.
19 Ibid.
20 DePrey, Nick (2016, July 8). "Minute by minute: How NPR uses listening data to make better radio." Podcast Movement presentation.
21 Ibid.
22 Levi, Ran (2016, Aug. 2). Skype interview.
23 Thompson, Caitlin (2016, June 15). Phone interview.
24 Ibid.
25 Ibid.
26 Ibid.
27 Mosel, Sarah van (2016, May 31). Phone interview.
28 Ibid.

29 Nichols, Mary (2016, June 8). Skype interview.
30 Ibid.
31 Ibid.
32 Jackson, David (2016, Aug. 6). Skype interview.
33 Ibid.
34 Ibid.
35 Tan.
36 Ibid.
37 Ibid.
38 Dumas.
39 Ibid.

2

Setting Up Your Studio

A strange misunderstanding typically occurs when podcasters give advice to others about starting a podcast. Invariably, the newbie's first questions are "What equipment should I use to record my podcast? How do I edit the audio? How should I get it online? How can I get my podcast on iTunes?" Good questions all, but not the ones with which you should be starting out on your podcasting adventure.

Experienced podcasters know this. They've put the time in. They've made all the mistakes. So when you ask an experienced podcaster these questions, her response will be something like "Don't worry about the audio. Figure out what your podcast is about. Focus on who your audience is, and market it to them. Concentrate on your content. That's the most important thing about starting a podcast."

The takeaway for many new podcasters is usually "The audio is not that important."

But that's not what the experienced podcaster said.

Any podcaster who's been around for a while has learned that audio quality is extremely important. You can't expect people to listen to your podcast or even come back time and again if the audio experience is an ordeal—if the sound is too soft or too loud or if there's too much background noise.

"The role of knowing how to produce your audio is to provide a good experience for the listener. Period," said Chris Curran, longtime audio engineer, podcast producer and host of *The Podcast Engineering Show*. "You don't want them riding the volume knob, so that's why you learn how to do your levels properly to make the whole thing transparent for the listener. The listener shouldn't even be thinking about frequencies or levels or volume or audio engineering—nothing. The listener should be listening to the content."[1]

The technology available today to create listenable audio is not very complicated. We're not talking about super-smooth, radio-quality recording. We're talking the bare minimum sound experience. The barrier of entry to producing a good-sounding podcast is quite low, in fact.

"You don't need an audio engineer to listen to your podcast and say, 'Wow, this sound is amazing, man,'" Curran said. "You don't have to be amazing. You just have to be good. So there's like a minimum level of good that you have to be. You should be that, and you don't have to become an audio engineer either. You just need to learn what you need to learn to at least sound good. And then forget about it right then and focus on the content."[2]

Even the technical process of posting a podcast is not that difficult. Do you want to record a podcast and get it online in half an hour? You can. Take your smartphone recorder, use the internal microphone and a native recording app to record yourself, export the audio to your laptop—actually, if the app is set up properly you can skip this step altogether—and upload it to a free audio platform like SoundCloud. Add some text explaining what the audio is, add a few tags so it's searchable on Google and save it. Your podcast is now online.

Next, use SoundCloud's share function to share the audio over social media, and take the embeddable player and put it on your website. Then, go into the SoundCloud settings and grab your RSS feed. This is what you send to iTunes. Once Apple has tested the feed and approved your podcast, you'll show up in the iTunes store.

Boom. You're a podcaster.

If podcasting is this easy, then why are there so many websites, YouTube videos, books—yes, this one included—and schools teaching people how to do it?

FIGURE 2.1 You don't need an elaborate studio to do a podcast. With a microphone and the right software, you can record an episode on your smartphone.

Remember what Todd Cochrane of the Blubrry podcast hosting service said in Chapter 1. Podcasting is hard. Coming up with a concept that people want to listen to and return to can be a challenge. Those are all the big problems that you need to be putting your attention toward if you want long-term success. Audio quality is important—extremely important—but the more attention you can devote at the beginning to focusing on your content, the better off you'll be in the long run.

SOLVE YOUR TECHNICAL PROBLEMS EARLY, SO YOU CAN FOCUS ON YOUR CONTENT

When we launched *It's All Journalism*, we lucked out. We worked at a radio station that gave us unlimited access to thousands of dollars worth of broadcast-quality recording equipment. We had our choice of four studios from which to do our interviews. If a guest was in another city, we could call them on a Telos line that was patched into our soundboard. We had headphones, microphones and recording software free of charge. From the start, we had the luxury of not having to worry about creating audio.

This, however, created other problems that wouldn't become apparent until later. Early on, we made it a priority to get people into the studio to record, because we believed the interviews would be more entertaining and conversational than those done over the phone. This decision about producing quality content created a scheduling nightmare for us. Not only did we have to juggle our recording times around our guests' schedules, we had to plan around the three producers' schedules as well. This meant we had no set recording time. Inflexibility was hard-coded into our workflow.

Being a studio-bound podcast, we'd never noodled through the challenges of recording audio in the field. It wasn't until a year into the podcast that we got a chance to go out in the world and record episodes remotely. And when we did, the audio sucked. It sucked big time.

Fellow producer Megan Cloherty and I set up a table at the 2014 Online News Association conference in Chicago, with the aim of grabbing interviews with some of the media experts at the convention. Both she and I, in our day jobs, had done standup interviews with our iPhones or digital recorders, so we felt comfortable interviewing people on the fly.

For the convention, I'd purchased four Behringer microphones, a four-track mixer and an audio interface from Amazon. I also bought a set of 1/4-inch audio cables and four cheap sets of headphones from Guitar Center.

Before flying out to Chicago, I tested the setup in my bedroom, plugging the microphones into the mixer, running that through the audio interface and then hooking that up to my MacBook Pro laptop. I used Audacity audio software to test the signal and record my voice over the four microphones, making adjustments to each of the tracks with the mixer. Everything seemed to work fine. If there were any problems at the convention, we'd just wing it.

Arriving in Chicago, I discovered very early there were going to be problems. Our table was in the back of a cavernous conference room, right next to a loudspeaker. I set up our portable recording studio and determined the sound quality was OK, not great, as long as no one made any announcements.

When the convention got into full swing, though, things got much worse very quickly. The background noise nearly drowned out our guests' voices. Worse still, the cheap headphones I'd bought failed to cancel out the din. Our guests couldn't hear us, and we couldn't hear them. We muscled through the interviews over the next two days of recording, hoping they would sound all right after we tweaked the audio back at the studio.

We had hoped the episodes from the 2014 Online News Association conference would showcase our podcast to the people we envisioned would be our ideal audience. Instead, the episodes were a bust and, at best for us at least, a learning experience for future remote recordings.

Although the audio setup had been fine in my quiet bedroom, it failed miserably in a noisy convention hall. It wasn't so much a problem with the equipment; it was that the equipment was not right for the place I was recording in. I was in an environment that I couldn't control.

CONTROL YOUR ENVIRONMENT

A professional radio or television studio is designed to lessen the impact of the environment on the recording process. This is achieved through heavily padded doors, carpeted floors, double-paned glass and sound-dampening tiles on walls and ceilings.

Although podcasters don't have to build a professionally designed studio to record in, they do need to put some consideration into the space where they plan to record, in order to minimize background interference.

The type of podcast you're planning to produce dictates the type of studio you'll need to set up. Of course, "studio" refers to the space you record in. It doesn't have to be a separate, walled-off room. It could be your dining room table, garage or office, as long as there is enough space for the host, guests and recording equipment.

Look for a quiet place, one where you won't be disturbed by an intrusive roommate, a barking dog or the blaring sound of a television. Although it may be tempting to sit at the kitchen table to record, you should know that large appliances, such as refrigerators, can generate unexpected background noise.

Take control of the space. Is there anything you can do that would make it even quieter, like unplugging appliances or adding carpeting and drapes?

Once you've found a quiet space for your studio, consider what tools you'll need to populate it.

Familiarize yourself with the tools of the trade.

"When you're starting from scratch, there's a lot of options and there's a lot of ways to do things," Curran said. "The first thing [to] think about is are you going to be recording in person? Are you going to be out on the street with a microphone recording conversations? Are you going to be sitting at home in a 'studio,' which might just be your desk, or are you going to have people into your studio and sit across from each other and have a conversation and record that? Are you going to just connect with people over the internet, [using] Skype or something like that and record conversations that way?"[3]

Each of those different circumstances requires different equipment and a different setup.

"First you have to decide what you want to do," Curran said. "Probably a lot of people would say, 'Oh, I want to do all three of those.' Well, OK. Then there's a bunch of equipment involved. Microphones—if you're the only one sitting at your desk and you're going to be speaking to someone over Skype, then you only need one microphone. If someone's going to be sitting with you in the same room, then you need two microphones. Let's say you need two microphones. Where do you plug in the two mics? You need an audio interface, which is basically just a tiny piece of equipment that you plug your mics into and then [it] connects to your computer. You just open up a simple free recording program like Audacity, and you just record the two microphones, one on the left, one on the right."

For fledgling podcasters, trying to imagine all the scenarios in which they might find themselves recording a podcast can be overwhelming. How many microphones should you buy? Do you need a mixer?

The best approach, as with a lot of things in life, is to start out simply, master the equipment at hand, and add pieces as you go along. There's no rush to build a complex or expensive studio. In fact, the simpler you keep things, the easier it will be to master the audio recording process and maintain a degree of flexibility in different recording situations.

The basic podcast recording setup is for a single person to record his or her own voice and post it as a podcast episode. The example given earlier in this chapter of someone using a smartphone as a recorder fits that scenario. For the moment, though, let's delay the discussion of using smartphones or tablets and instead look at the key tools in a podcaster's toolbox. It'll be easier to demonstrate how to expand your toolbox as your podcast grows.

Go to Appendix B, "Shopping Guide," to view equipment, services and software used by some of the podcasters who served as sources for this book.

Microphones

Although podcasters have an endless number of online experts to answer questions and retailers to buy merchandise from, it's worthwhile to visit a local music outlet to do some field research on recording equipment. Podcasting may be relatively new, but musicians have been recording digital audio for years. The more established businesses will most likely have someone on staff who can answer your questions and explain the uses of the different types of microphones, mixers, audio interfaces and so on.

In the Washington, DC, area, Chuck Levin's Music Center has been selling musical instruments and recording equipment since 1958. Adam Levin, grandson of the store's founder, has advised musicians and podcasters on audio recording. He recommends that new podcasters start out using a cardioid microphone.[4]

Cardioid refers to the pattern of sound the microphone records. Unlike an omnidirectional microphone, which records in all directions, a cardioid

FIGURE 2.2 Adam Levin, grandson of the founder of Chuck Levin's Music in Wheaton, Maryland, advises musicians and podcasters on audio recording.

records in only one direction. Shotgun mics—those long, thin microphones that you sometimes see TV reporters pointing at their subjects—are an example of a cardioid microphone. The tightly focused recording pattern makes it easier to differentiate the speaker's voice from the surrounding noise.

The downside of the cardioid microphone is that, with its limited recording area, the speaker needs to be talking directly into the microphone to get the best sound. If a speaker drifts from side to side or turns his or her head, the volume will rise and fall. At Federal News Radio, where I work, the news anchors tell guests to position themselves about a fist's length from the microphone to ensure that their voices are recorded properly.

A new podcaster may be tempted to buy one omnidirectional mic and put it in the middle of a table to record a podcast. That way he or she can save money on microphones and record everybody at once.

I'd advise against this for a couple of reasons. First, everyone's voice will be recorded at different levels. Somebody sitting farther from the microphone won't sound as clear or as loud as someone closer in. Second, and more importantly, all voices will be recorded on the same audio track. The person in charge of the recording won't be able to make adjustments to the levels of each speaker, and the person editing the audio after the recording is completed won't be able to match levels during post-production.

The omnidirectional microphone may seem easier and better at capturing that "it's just a bunch of friends hanging out" vibe, but trust me, it's a limiting factor. The audio won't sound as good, and it'll be harder to fix later on. Everyone who is going to speak on a podcast should have their own microphone. Everyone.

"In the world of microphones, there's really two types of microphones," Levin said. "There's condensers and there's dynamics. Dynamics are most of the microphones that you see that they have that ball on top; that's a handheld microphone. It's like a speaker in reverse. It's a lot less sensitive than a studio microphone. They can take a beating; you can throw it in your bag; they can handle moisture. They're fairly rugged. They're meant for live [recording]. So this is the mic you see on stage in a rock concert."[5]

These are the types of microphones you'll also see used for panel discussions and at conferences.

"It's not the type of microphone you often see in a recording studio or a broadcast studio," Levin said. "But, because it's less sensitive, that means you're automatically rejecting some extraneous sounds. [You're] probably not going to get people's hands clicking on the table or papers rustling. You're going to be really directed on the source. As a novice, I'd say focus on that, because it's going to make the rest of your life a lot easier when you're not picking up junk. You're getting exactly what you want to hear."

Condenser microphones are much more sensitive and are usually what you'll find in a professional recording studio.

"These have a very, very, very thin piece of metal in there that's electrified from a source, like a preamp or something," Levin said. "Because they're so sensitive and they're so light, they pick up every little detail of your voice, but also anything else that is going on. Even though it's cardioid and they may have a reflection point, it's still going to hear it, because sound is everywhere. You can use those microphones, in a way, in a controlled situation, if you have a recording studio or a bedroom where you can control the sound. Let's say I was trying to record in my bedroom and my neighbor turned on the laundry machine—you'll hear that in the recording, and that can just totally crap the whole thing out."[6]

Although condensers may sound better than dynamics, their sensitivity makes them a less than ideal choice for someone just starting out in audio production. You want a microphone that's forgiving and one you can knock around a bit as you're learning the ropes.

"A lot of people want to get into podcasting without knowing too much about recording, and generally they don't think that it's necessary to have a recording studio, but it really is," Levin said. "That's what you're doing. You have to be able to record a good source cleanly, without picking up extraneous sounds, and edit it in a way that the end result sounds nice, clean and pleasant. Working with the dynamic will make your life a lot easier in the beginning, until you can grow to a point where your editing chops and your recording chops and all that sort of stuff is up to par, where if you did introduce a higher quality microphone that might be a little more difficult to work with, you know what you're doing at that point. Also, dynamics tend to be a little bit less expensive."[7]

Once you've chosen a microphone, be sure to purchase a foam windscreen to put over it. This will help deaden sharp vocal sounds, usually described as "popping your p's".

Headphones

Podcasters and their guests should always wear headphones. Wearing headphones helps everyone involved hear what's being recorded and monitor their own voice. They'll be able to match their volume with the other speakers and know when to move up if they're too far from the microphone. It will also make it easier for them to keep track of the flow of the conversation and hear the questions being asked.

Never trust the display on your computer or digital recorder. Learn to trust your ears. If someone sounds too low or too loud, make an adjustment so that his or her voice balances with the other speakers.

"For headphones in the podcast arena, closed-back headphones should be where we're looking," Levin said. "In general, there are three types of headphones, and we're talking about over-your-ear headphones, not buds. There's open back, semi-open back and closed back. The first two are going to be used in your more studio-mixing scenarios. You'll actually see perforations or holes on the outside of the headphone, which might give you a more pleasing sound when you're listening for mixing, but they let sound out. So if you're in front of a mic, that's bled into the mic, so that could cause some anomalies that you don't necessarily want."[8]

In a monitoring situation, open-back headphones allow outside noise to get in and interfere with your ability to listen to the sound being recorded.

"You're not getting isolation, and you're also allowing for bleed into your microphone," Levin said. "So, closed back is going to be a solid shell, and that's going to, in most situations, passively prevent sound from coming in. When I say passively, I mean not noise-canceling headphones. It's passively allowing sound to block out extraneous sound from coming in, and it's keeping the sound that's inside your headphones in and not letting it bleed out. It's kind of like putting a wall between what you actually want to be hearing [and what you don't]. You want to hear exactly what's being captured. You don't want to hear that person's actual voice."[9]

Levin advises against using noise-canceling headphones.

"It might mess up with what you think you're really hearing," he said. "The best [choice] is just to go with a good set of closed-back headphones. They generally will isolate enough, and you want something that's fairly flat. You want to hear what you're actually capturing, so 'flat' is kind of the term that we use to describe something that's honest."[10]

If you purchase the right type of closed-back headphones, you can use them for both the recording side and the editing side of the production process.

"In the music community, if someone was mixing on, let's say, Beats headphones—those have a specific characteristic to them, really boosted lows, really boosted highs and makes for a pleasing musical experience," Levin said. "But if I recorded my voice and I'm like, 'Man, my voice sounds like the voice of God,' and 'Man, does that bass sound good,' I'm going to take that—I'm going to put it to a podcast, get it out there in the world, and it's going to sound thin, because when you listen on your computer or other headphones, they don't have that exaggerated bass. But I made my decisions based on that exaggerated bass."[11]

In other words, the best headphones for you to use in podcasting are not necessarily ones that deliver a "top of the line" listening experience. Levin recommends going into a store to test out several different pairs of headphones, listening to a familiar song on each until you find the one that delivers the most honest sound.

"I'd say the sweet spot is really between $89 and $149," he said. "[You can find] plenty of industry standard, great headphones in that price range. There's no need to go to $300, $400, $500 for what we're talking about. You can get by with headphones that are $50 or $60. But, if you really want something that's going to be good—you can trust it no matter what level of professionalism you're at—$89 to $149 is really good."[12]

Audio Cables

Audio cables may not seem that important, but they're an integral part of your recording setup.

"You could spend all the money in the world on the greatest microphone on the planet, and if you said, 'Yeah, I just need a cable just to get by,' you just wasted all that money. Your audio chain is only as good as your weakest link," Levin said. "Cable is like pipes in a water line. If your source is an awesome microphone, it wants to throw a lot of water down this pipeline. And if you only give it a tiny little cable that's all corroded and terrible, very little of it is going to get through. You want to give it the best pipeline you can. A better cable is going to allow more signal, clearer or better. You'd be surprised at how much a cable can mess up the sound of something, and ultimately it's either what's being recorded or what you're listening to. That the cable can affect it could ruin everything."[13]

He suggests choosing a balanced cable over an unbalanced cable, because balanced cables shield the audio signal from outside interference better, eliminating unwanted clicks and hums created by intruding radio frequencies.

Levin also says to use XLR cables instead of 1/4-inch audio cables to hook up your microphones to your recording equipment. XLR cables have round, cupped ends with three-pronged (male) connectors or three-holed (female) connectors to better lock into devices.

Recording Devices

In the basic recording setup, the beginning podcaster starts out with one microphone hooked up to a recording device. The recording device may be a digital recorder, a tablet, a smartphone or even a laptop.

After the Chicago journalism conference fiasco, I purchased a Zoom H4n digital recorder to do recording in the field. It has two built-in microphones, which are great in a pinch for a quick standup interview. But I prefer to use one or two dynamic microphones that I can plug into the H4n with XLR cables. Unfortunately, the H4n has just one headphone input. But a headphone splitter allows both the interviewer and the interviewee to monitor the recording.

Digital recorders, like the Zoom H4n and the Tascam DR-40, aren't just for recording out in the field. They can also be used in a studio setting with two microphones on stands plugged directly into the recorder.

Neal Augenstein, my colleague at WTOP radio in Washington, DC, has been using an iPhone to record all of his audio since 2010. Not only does he cover the news and file daily audio features, he produced the five-part *The Hannah Graham Story* podcast for CBS News' "48 Hours."

FIGURE 2.3 In this scenario, the podcaster is using two microphones plugged into a digital recorder. Note: Both participants should be wearing headphones to ensure that the audio sounds great.

Initially, Augenstein turned to the iPhone as a way to streamline his reporting process and unburden himself of all the extraneous equipment he had to cart around, like a camera, a digital recorder, microphones and a laptop.

"The reason why I did it on the iPhone was that there was a multitrack audio editing app that would allow me to record it and to immediately begin editing it," he said. "I thought that would save some time. I wasn't sure the audio quality would be sufficient. I did some field testing. I found out, in my opinion, that the audio was 92 percent as good as if I were using a digital recorder with a field microphone. After weighing all the pros and cons, I found that [with] the speed and the ease of use and the fact that I could share that audio on several platforms, it was worth it for me. And the audience at home was not able to distinguish the difference between the sound quality of the iPhone and the digital recorder."[14]

When Augenstein goes out in the field, he packs a small kit: iPhone, iPad, a couple of chargers and a $3 windscreen he purchased from Amazon. This last item he slips over the end of the iPhone to cover the built-in microphone.

FIGURE 2.4 For a more mobile studio setup, connect a dynamic microphone to an iPhone or iPad using the IK Multimedia iRig Pro Audio/MIDI Interface. IK Multimedia also makes microphones that connect directly to iPhones with a jack to plug your headphones into.

These days, Augenstein uses the Ferrite mobile app to record and edit almost all of his audio. He also has access to Adobe Audition software so that he can edit audio at his desk if he needs to.

"It's a relatively intuitive app that is designed for journalists or people who are familiar with multitrack audio editing software," Augenstein said. "One of the things I like about it is that it looks similar to the audio editing software that I use on a desktop." However, he noted: "It's a bit pricey for somebody who is just starting. There are cheaper or free desktop software that they can use."[15]

With the free version of Ferrite that Augenstein uses in the field, he can separate cuts out of the raw audio, put them on one track and add a voiceover on another. "Maybe I'll put some natural sound on track 3 and then I can mix them all down together into a single report, a single mono report or stereo report," he said. "I can share that with my newsroom in a variety of ways, (either) through email; you can Dropbox it, tweet the audio or put it on Facebook."[16]

Not every podcaster needs to be as mobile as a radio reporter, but podcasters might want to take advantage of the flexibility that smartphones and tablets offer.

"I think it's a perfectly valid recording medium, [one that works] just as well as a portable recorder," said Levin. "There are even microphones that you can use that plug into your phone to give you better sound than the built-in mic."[17]

iRig manufactures a handheld condenser microphone that can be used with Apple and Android devices. Other styles of microphones can be connected to these devices via an XLR cable using the IK Multimedia iRig Pro Audio/MIDI Interface.

"The built-in mic on your phone is going to pick up all kinds of sound in all different ways," Levin said. "It's not necessarily directional, but there are peripheral microphones that you can add to an iPhone or an Android device that can give you a handheld dynamic microphone to use that is directional, so that you're not picking up the whole room. You're just picking up your source."[18]

Smartphones and tablets also work well with lavaliers, those small, omnidirectional microphones you see pinned to guests on television panel shows.

"There are lavalier microphones that you can use that plug into your phone to give you superior audio quality, to just have in your pocket as you're going around making notes or doing the recordings, [which is] better than holding your phone right up to your mouth," Levin said.[19]

The Blue Yeti USB microphone, which offers three recording patterns (cardioid, omnidirectional and bidirectional), comes with a USB cable you can plug directly into your computer. You can then open audio production software, like Audacity, Adobe Audition, Cubase Studio, GarageBand, Hindenburg or Pro Tools, to record your audio track.

It's a pretty no-fuss, no-muss solution, recording directly into the program you're already going to use to edit the audio file. All the software titles mentioned here allow for multitrack recording. But what if you want to interview a guest and add more microphones?

"When you're recording to a computer, you now have a virtual mixer in your computer with an unlimited channel count," Levin said. "So where you might have been confined to two channels on your recorder with no effects and no routing and other things that you can do, going into the computer realm opens up a world of possibilities. The device that you would need there is called an audio interface. This is going to be much like your portable recorder. How many things do you want to record simultaneously—one, two, four, eight, sixteen channels into your computer with the USB cable and all coming into your computer individually separated?"[20]

There is no one right solution for recording a podcast. Be adaptable.

Some studio setups are easy: Just you, a microphone and a recorder. Others require a bit more creative thinking, like having your hosts live thousands of miles away from each other.

That's the problem BuzzFeed producer Julia Furlan faced with the *Internet Explorer* podcast. Whereas host Katie Notopoulos lives in New York City, co-host Ryan Broderick recently moved to Great Britain.

"I, as a producer, had to solve the problem of what do you do when one host is literally in a different country, a different time zone?" Furlan said. "We've done a lot of different versions of this, and we've sort of experimented. Ultimately, when you're producing something, the production has its own personality, and, like the production, how you produce a show has its own way of adapting to the people around it and the people who are making it."[21]

When *Internet Explorer* first launched, the producers didn't have the budget to create two studios.

"Ryan would record it in a studio [in Great Britain] with Katie in a studio here in New York, and we synced up via Skype so they could see each other," Furlan said. "Then I built out a little room in a closet at BuzzFeed, and essentially Ryan started recording the podcast. He's very technically proficient, like he's a musician."[22]

Furlan sent Broderick a Studio S1B microphone and a Tascam DR-60 recorder to record himself.

"And then Katie, in this recording room, we would sync up using FaceTime or Skype," she said. "We would use Skype for them to see each other, and I set up an iPad on a stand, so that they would be looking at each other and record Katie with a Studio Projects B1 (microphone) and [Zoom H6] recorder. We would have guests in this room too."[23]

When the recording is finished, Broderick sends his audio file to Furlan, who syncs it with the audio she recorded in studio, editing it using Hindenburg Journalist Pro.

Furlan started out producing podcasts at WNYC, the New York City NPR radio station, before joining BuzzFeed. She takes audio production seriously and strives to ensure every episode of *Internet Explorer* reflects this professional attention to detail.

"If you listen to it, I think you could tell that somebody took care to produce it," she said. "I think it sounds really good. And that is something that we have always said at BuzzFeed Audio. Collectively as a group, we believe that good, well recorded, technically proficient audio is part of how we think, how we put things in the world. The same way you don't put an article out with typos."

Furlan's years of experience allowed her to take advantage of the flexibility today's audio technology affords the podcaster in order to solve her particular recording challenge.

This is something that every podcaster can accomplish over time. You can talk into your smartphone or work in a professional studio with 16 microphones and a giant soundboard. Start out simply, master each step and grow.

ACTIVITIES

1. What will be the format of your podcast? Will you be talking into a microphone by yourself, or will you be recording interviews? Will it be a storytelling podcast with multiple elements? Plan out where and how you will be recording your podcast. Do you have access to a studio, or will you be creating one in your home or workspace? Identify the space you'll be using, paying attention to how much ambient noise can be heard.

2. Make a shopping list of the recording equipment you'll need: Microphones, microphone stands, windscreens, XLR cables and headphones. [See Appendix B.] Will you be recording on your computer? If so, you'll need an audio interface or a microphone that plugs directly into your computer via a USB cable. You'll also need software to edit the audio. If you go the digital recorder, smartphone or tablet route, make a list of the equipment and software you'll need to support that choice. Then, go online to price all the equipment and make a budget.

3. With your shopping list in hand, visit an electronics or music store that carries digital recording supplies. If possible, try out microphones, headphones and any other equipment you can. Also, ask store personnel what type of recording equipment they recommend for recording a podcast. This is just a fact-finding mission. You don't need to purchase anything. Just familiarize yourself with the equipment and make the best choices for your budget.

NOTES

1 Curran, Chris (2016, Aug. 17). Phone interview.
2 Ibid.
3 Ibid.
4 Levin, Adam (2016, July 5). Personal interview.
5 Ibid.
6 Ibid.
7 Ibid.
8 Ibid.
9 Ibid.
10 Ibid.
11 Ibid.
12 Ibid.
13 Ibid.
14 Augenstein, Neal (2016, May 16). Personal interview.

15 Ibid.
16 Ibid.
17 Levin.
18 Ibid.
19 Ibid.
20 Ibid.
21 Furlan, Julia (2016, June 10). Phone interview.
22 Ibid.
23 Ibid.

3

Preparing for Your First Episode

Now that you've decided what type of podcast you want to do, identified an audience and figured out how to record audio, it's time to think about planning that first episode. This is a chance to establish a work structure that will carry you forward week to week and ensure you'll produce a quality podcast on time and with regularity.

One of the things I enjoy most about talking to other podcasters is hearing an idea that makes me say to myself: "That's so obvious! Why didn't I think of that?"

Recently, I was in Minneapolis for work and had the chance to talk to Phil Mackey, a columnist for 1500ESPN.com and co-host of the Mackey & Judd radio show. We were discussing a project he was involved in, recruiting local talent who wanted to podcast. One of the problems he encountered was that, although plenty of people had an idea for a podcast, very few knew what they wanted to do after the first couple of episodes. His solution? If someone wanted to pitch him a podcast, they had to include detailed ideas for the first five episodes. That way, he could weed out the wannabes and deal only with those who were serious about producing an ongoing podcast.[1]

Great idea, right? I wish I'd thought of it back in 2012 when we launched *It's All Journalism*. At the beginning, we had next to no content planning.

We knew our format—interviewing digital journalists about how they did their jobs—and how we were going to record, but we didn't have any topics mapped out or a lengthy guest list. Our first few episodes were conversations with friends or professors from graduate school.

But that was OK. We were learning the ropes. There's nothing wrong with starting a podcast talking to a few friends and colleagues. You're going to have a rough enough time figuring out how to set the microphone levels as you try to maintain an engaging conversation—why not make it easy on yourself?

However, creating a detailed plan of what the first five or so episodes are going to be about will help you think about the structure of your podcast and how much preparation you'll need. Jot down a list of topics and guests.

The next thing you need to do is get some people to help you. Oh, and make sure you hire a producer.

PODCASTING IS MORE FUN WITH MORE PEOPLE; DIVIDE THE WORK

When I say, "Hire a producer," I don't mean you have to "hire a producer." Chances are, initially you'll be doing your podcast on the cheap and won't have money to pay them anyway. Instead, look for like-minded individuals who want to podcast who can share the workload and help develop your content. But somebody—maybe it's you—needs to be the show's producer, the person who's going to follow an episode from the grain of an idea through the production and post-production process, ensuring that a high level of quality is being maintained.

"I think the role of a podcaster/radio producer is such a wide term, and 'producer' means so many different things in so many different industries," said Gina Delvac, producer of the *Call Your Girlfriend* podcast. "For people who are familiar with, say, the magazine or writing profession, it's a person who's like an editor, both in the sense of having the ability to edit audio files but also to really share ideas. It's that person who's looking out for blind spots in your perspective who can say, 'Hey, why don't we try this?' "[2]

Most of Delvac's experience in audio production came from working in public radio, in particular as a producer for American Public Media and Southern California Public Media. After that, she was an executive producer at Launch Media, LLC, overseeing the twice-weekly *This Week in Startups* podcast.

She developed *Call Your Girlfriend* with co-hosts—and real-life best friends—Ann Friedman and Aminatou Sow. The podcast's goal and part of its appeal, according to Delvac, is that it's a "conversation between two friends who both happened to be in their early 30s."[3]

"The heart of the show is conversation, and then we have always wanted to highlight other women who are doing great work," Delvac said. "And again, always from kind of that cauldron of friendship."[4]

The three-sided nature of their working relationship proved to be a recipe for success.

"People talk about . . . tripartite relationships being very problematic and difficult," Delvac said.

> For us, it's been great in terms of dividing the workload. We each have things that we can specialize in, and it kind of diffuses any sense of, in a two-way partnership, who's pulling more weight. You run into the problems that you hear of old married couples. "I'm always the one washing the dishes," but it's a work sense of like, "Why do I always have to do all this stuff?" It can feel unbalanced. And so in our case, I'm the person who is in charge of everything sound-related and sometimes planning, of being the off-the-mic person who can give that critical or honest feedback that we talked about before.[5]

The three-way division of labor allows Delvac to concentrate on improving the technical side of producing a biweekly podcast.

"Ann and Amina can really focus on things that they're great at together, which include editorial qualities, like story selection and thinking about their opinions, and sort of channeling that deep friendship . . . to just bounce ideas off one another," Delvac said.

> Amina is—professionally, she's a digital strategist. She's amazing at marketing. So that's something that she frequently works on. Ann was an editor at a magazine for many years, so she's incredibly talented in that area. [She is] super organized, puts together the best outlines

and can hack together a PowerPoint presentation deck better than anyone's ever seen in such a short time.[6]

The three-sided work flow, in the end, plays to each of their strengths. Delvac says:

> For them [Ann and Amina], a producer is the person who can help you with ideas, who can speak out about sound, if they want to go in that direction, or who can just help offload some of the work. It just makes the creative and fruitful partnerships that much more exciting, as long as you all feel equally invested in the project. That's always the hard part.[7]

EPISODE TOPICS SHOULD SERVICE THE BROADER MISSION

Jennifer Crawford spearheads the planning behind *The JellyVision Show*, a weekly discussion-style podcast about entrepreneurship in the creative arts. With backgrounds in comedy and improv, Crawford and her co-host Tim Trueheart keep the banter light and entertaining. Though comedy may come naturally for them, they have to put some thought into every episode to ensure that it's informative too. Crawford says:

> Being consistent and planning—we know it's important, because we've done it and we haven't done it. And sometimes it's a hybrid of both. But in terms of prep, we now choose a topic for a show and then we'll research that topic. We can read about other people's points of view, other factual elements and then digest that and then come up with our own take. Then when we have a guest, we will know enough about the guest that we can introduce them and know [from] their background whether they are enough of a good fit for the show. But we don't overly research them, because we also want to be naturally curious about them when we do talk to them on the show.[8]

The key to good planning is matching discussion points and guests to the broader mission of the podcast. With Crawford and Trueheart, for example, they look for topics that fit under the umbrella of entrepreneurship. Crawford says:

> We might talk about mentors, and we may just research the heck out of that topic so that we know the different kinds of mentors, what

FIGURE 3.1 Author Michael O'Connell, center, poses for a photo with _The JellyVision Show_ hosts Tim Trueheart and Jennifer Crawford.

to look for in a mentor, what to avoid in a mentor, why you want to mentor. That might be something that we could fill an episode with.[9]

Once Crawford completes her research, she writes up her notes and shares them with her co-host so he can prepare for the recording. Trueheart says:

> She sends me this email. Here's the guest and then here's a couple of links, so I'm going to click on the link see the guy's social media presence. If he's on Twitter I'm like: "Hooray, I love Twitter. Follow." I'll follow him and add him to a list. I'll check out a couple quick links or skim a page. I want to get a sense of doing it like this. If you have nothing, then you're a little lost, really, walking on a wooden bridge across two cliffs.[10]

STRUCTURE CAN EASE THE PLANNING PROCESS

Podcasters Nigel Poor, Earlonne Woods and Antwan Williams know something about working within a structure. The three are developing _Ear Hustle_, a podcast documenting life inside San Quentin State Prison in California.

Poor, a professor of photography, came to San Quentin in 2011 as part of the Prison University Project, the only onsite degree-granting program in the California Department of Corrections and Rehabilitation. Poor says:

> One of my students, named Troy Williams, who was incarcerated at San Quentin at that time, wanted to work on a documentary film about life inside prison, and he asked if I would help him. We started working on it, and it became apparent that doing film in there was going to be incredibly difficult because we'd have to do all the editing inside, and so we decided to just do audio interviews. From there, a local San Francisco station, KALW, heard about what we were doing and got interested and said they would be interested in airing programs if we actually started producing stories. They sent in people to train us on all aspects of radio development, and, in 2013, we started airing our stories on the KALW show "Crosscurrents."[11]

For her next audio project, Poor wanted to do something with more sound design and longer storytelling. She started developing *Ear Hustle* with Woods, a 42-year-old serving a life sentence.

Poor says:

> Since he's been incarcerated, on his own, he's studied filmmaking and radio, and he's got a wonderful voice and he's a great writer. We wanted to co-host something together. The idea was to really concentrate on an inside and outside project, where incarcerated and non-incarcerated people can work together in a real collaborative way. He just has that kind of spirit. He's just somebody you want to be around and work with. He's very talented.[12]

Poor and Woods were joined by their sound designer, Antwan Williams, who has been incarcerated for 10 years and possesses, according to Poor, a "very keen ear."

> San Quentin is an unusual prison in that there's a lot of programs there, very interesting programs. They've been publishing a newspaper there, I think, for like 28 years. They have an educational program. They have a Shakespeare group that comes in there and does plays and they have a—actually a nice media center. We have Mac computers.

FIGURE 3.2 *Ear Hustle* producers, from left, Antwan Williams, Nigel Poor and Earlonne Woods record their podcast in San Quentin Prison.

We actually have Pro Tools in there. We have microphones and film cameras. That's where we work, and all of the interviewing, all the editing happens inside that media lab.[13]

Before Poor can take the audio out and post it online, she has to submit it to the prison's public relations officer for approval.

After we get edited down, I can take it out. He can listen to it, but we could never take out three hours of raw footage, because he'd have to listen to everything and that's just not going to happen.[14]

In March 2016, Radiotopia announced the Podquest contest, in which one or more winners would have their podcast picked up by the network. From the 1,537 entries, *Ear Hustle* was one of the contest's four finalists, and so Williams, Poor and Woods were invited to appear at the July 6–8 Podcast Movement conference in Chicago. When I interviewed Poor there, she said the first eight episodes had already been mapped out.

We're going to do one about cooking in prison. How you turn your cell into a kitchen and how you get ingredients in a place that is very devoid of any nourishing sustenance. We're doing a story about the minister who goes onto death row to minister to the condemned men there. We're doing a story about how the N-word is used in prison by different races. I want to do a story about prison fashion: There's obviously a uniform that people have to wear, but everybody, I think, has this internal sense of wanting to stand out and be an individual. I'm really interested in how men do that to this state-issued uniform.[15]

What Poor finds most thrilling about *Ear Hustle* is its peek inside a world most of us have never seen.

I'm always curious about going someplace new and being challenged and having my assumptions changed. Of course before I went into prison, my mind really only saw it as a place that was sculpted by what I read in the newspaper and what I see in movies and such. To go in there and just see such a different world and to meet men that have done some terrible things and are in the process of rehabilitating themselves is fascinating to me.[16]

Standup comedian Zahra Noorbakhsh and her friend Tanzila "Taz" Ahmed, who is a writer, activist and politico, started their podcast *Good Muslim Bad Muslim* as something of an inside joke. It grew out of the social media musings of two Muslim-American women living in a post-9/11 America.

> Taz and I had actually been going back and forth on Twitter, sort of in jest, claiming "good Muslim, bad Muslim," and then we started just like doing the hashtag all together—#goodmuslimbadmuslim—because sometimes it wasn't clear if we were doing a good thing or a bad thing. There was no winning either way. And then the more and more we would sort of joke back and forth on Twitter with that hashtag, the more often it came out that it was like we were losing no matter what. Either you're a good Muslim within the Muslim community or bad Muslim outside the Muslim community. You kind of can't win.[17]

It was during these exchanges that they began pretending they had an actual podcast.

> We would say, "On our next *Good Muslim Bad Muslim Podcast*" and just kind of joke about it, and we did that for a year. And after a year of just kind of joking about it, we started to get people saying, "Hey, I went to go look up your podcast—where is it?"[18]

The more Noorbakhsh and Ahmed thought about it, the more they realized launching a podcast might not be a bad idea.

> At that time, the technology was still a little too technical for us to pick up on. And in the second year, we saw that, actually, this is something that we could feasibly do, because she and I are in different cities. I'm in San Francisco, she's in Los Angeles, and so we also weren't sure how that was going to work.[19]

Eventually, they were able to surmount the distance issue with the help of Skype and a little diligence in their episode planning for their monthly recording sessions.

> We used to try to do the agenda three days in advance, just because it would be stressful to try to do it beforehand. But instead, we just got faster at our communication beforehand, because the news cycle as it relates to Muslims is changing by the hour, and it's really hard to keep up with. And so, we try to match our agenda to the episode as close as

possible, and we go through it, and all month we post links to articles and say, "Next time on the *#GoodMuslimBadMuslim Podcast*."[20]

As they planned out their podcast, Noorbakhsh and Ahmed developed a structure built around regular segments, such as "Creeping Sharia" and "All the Ways We're Winning." They also handed out Good Muslim Awards and issued fatwas, all in good fun, of course. The segment structure eased the planning process by giving them regular slots to fill each episode. It also provided inspiration for listeners to contribute via social media.

We get a lot of our content because of fans who will tag us and send us links to articles saying, "Next time in 'Creeping Sharia'" or "Next time this should be a 'Fatwa,'" or "Are you guys going to talk about . . .?" That's one place where I'm glad that we're monthly, because I do feel like to react to the news as two Muslim women in conversation would be a sucky podcast. It doesn't afford us the opportunity to actually see the arc of the news cycle on a topic and think about what our experience is after that. Everything is sort of reactionary, and there isn't really a whole lot of time to actually formulate your thoughts and opinions when everything is unfolding by the hour, by the day.[21]

Comedians Dave Coulter and Kat Jessup's weekly podcast, *It's Advice! with Dave and Kat*, has a loose structure that helps serve its humorous intent.

"The focus is I'll be drunk and give well-meaning advice," Coulter said.

"I think the tagline is 'Well-intentioned, if boozy, advice,'" Jessup said.

"The thing we say is: 'We give advice. You listen, stupid,'" Coulter said.[22]

Each episode follows a similar formula.

"There's an opening, and we have some patter and then we answer three questions and then we say what we learned today," Jessup said. "Then we beg people to send us more questions and then there's a bump at the end."[23]

Some questions take only two minutes to answer, but others take much longer to work out.

Sometimes we go into some deep dive about somebody who had a story from their childhood and 12 minutes later, OK, we start

FIGURE 3.3 **Comedians Dave Coulter and Kat Jessup are the hosts of**
It's Advice! with Dave and Kat.

answering questions in context. It can go either way, but it gives us a
general roadmap of where we want to go.[24]

Through good planning and time commitment, Jay Jacksonrao, host of *The
Nerdpocalypse* podcast, grew his interest in the medium into something
much larger than a single show.

I was a big podcast listener, which I still am, and I just decided with my
best friend that it would be really cool. We thought, "Hey, these other
shows that we listened to, they were able to do it, and why couldn't
we?" And we had some interest in doing a show specifically about sort
of nerd culture and movies and things that we grew up with and were
really passionate about, so we decided to give it a try. It just kind of
started out as a hobby really.[25]

Jacksonrao's hobby eventually grew into a business. He became the founder
and president of TNP Studios, a podcast network based in Baltimore, Maryland.

I have a podcast called *The Nerdpocalypse*, which is a movie/comic-
book nerds show. I also have another show, *Black on Black Cinema*,
which is a show specifically about films in the African-American

diaspora. There's another show, *Dense Pixels*, which is solely focused on video games and video game news and reviews. There is also another program we have called *Look Forward*, which is a political podcast, and we also have a show called *The Airing of Grievances*, which is a "Seinfeld" show. We also have a monthly show called *No Time to Bleed*, which is about action movies of the '70s, '80s and '90s. And then lastly, we have a show called *The Men with the Golden Tongues*, which is a James Bond–centric podcast.[26]

Before each weekly recording session for *The Nerdpocalypse*, Jacksonrao and his co-hosts Micah Payne, Jack Rous and Terrence Carpenter assemble a docket of topics they'll discuss, including links to relevant content.

Basically, we have sections for science and tech, and we have a couple of little fun segments that we do. We have a section called "Our Question of the Week Responses." We post a question a week on our Facebook page for our fans; they respond to that question, which is about something in the previous episode to give their idea on what did you think of this or what would you have done here or what is your show/movie idea or what have you?[27]

As a comic book–focused podcast, *The Nerdpocalypse* also has segments devoted to comic-book news and discussions of what the hosts are currently reading.

Then we have a section we just started . . . called "The Lightning Round," which is movie news that's really fast and we don't really have to get into it. So-and-so was cast in this movie, or this movie is moving from date X to date Y. Then we have the big bulk of our show, which is the movie and TV section, where we talk about the big news that's relevant to the show in the movie and television industry, whether there's a larger conversation about a certain comic book or larger conversation about a new TV show that's starting or something that's moving nights or something larger.[28]

As with Noorbakhsh and Ahmed, good planning around regular segments helps Jacksonrao streamline his podcast. It also helps provide content for the show's website when he releases an episode.

We post our docket. Our docket is broken out in those categories, and so they're all links, and they're typed out, and everything is linked.

When people see our WTF stories or they see some article that we mentioned, they know that they can go to our site, go to that particular episode, and they can read our docket and click on the link exactly in the docket. Literally, I copy and paste out of the docket that we use so they can see exactly the docket that we have.[29]

STRUCTURE IS NOT A SHACKLE

A simple structure helped Panoply plan and launch the pilot episode of one of the network's most successful podcasts—*Happier with Gretchen Rubin*.

"Their show was one of the first ones that kind of signed on to be part of the Panoply Network, and we had a first episode of their show live when we launched," said Laura Mayer, managing producer of the network.

> Gretchen and Liz Craft, her sister, came to Andy Bowers [Panoply's chief content officer] at some point before Panoply launched and before I started and said: "Hey, I'm an author who has a big audience. I've been writing about happiness and habits, and I'm interested in doing a show about that. Also, I want to spend more time with my sister, and, because we have very divergent takes on how to live our lives, we think it would be fun to do a podcast together, so that [we] could discuss things." So that was the initial pitch.[30]

Panoply decided to produce a pilot and assigned a producer to manage it.

> A lot of the times when we do a pilot, it'll work out really well, and that will end up being the first episode of the show. A lot of times, however, it will end up being a learning experience, where you realize something doesn't really work out. Gretchen was a very special case. She and Liz are incredibly organized pros. They came in with the show idea. They had kind of an outline that they had created based on sort of a script that we had given them.[31]

The outline Panoply gave Rubin and Craft to start with followed the structure of other *Slate* podcasts.

The outline had three segments, Mayer said.

> It's not like we wrote it for them, but it was sort of like: "This is where the intro would go. This is where you would do your first segment. This

is where you would close out the segment, throw to an ad if there's an ad there and remind people who you are and where to subscribe."[32]

Mayer was on hand for the recording of "One Minute Rule," the first episode of *Happier with Gretchen Rubin*:

They came in with the sort-of-loose outline. Gretchen, at the beginning, had scripted a lot of it, and the producer and I sat there in the recording [booth] to kind of help them when they got off track, make suggestions of how they could do things better, that sort of thing.[33]

In the end, the podcast was edited down to 20 minutes—the shortest episode of the series.

In terms of the continued development of the show, Gretchen and Liz, and this is true of all of our podcasters, they weren't interested in doing the exact same thing every week. They were interested in adding new segments, having guests, doing interviews, kind of changing up the format. Whenever they had that idea, either it was the kind of thing we would pitch to them, saying, "Hey, why don't you try this?" Or they would come to us and say, "Hey, I'm really interested in doing our first interview show, but I'm not exactly sure how to fit it into the format of the shows that we've already done." Then our producer and Andy and I would work with them to try and figure out a way that they could still stay true to how their show originally started but also kind of expand the way that they are doing it.[34]

Segmenting helped *Happier with Gretchen Rubin* find its structure but didn't shackle the show's producers. It provided them with a launching pad to take the show in new directions.

This particular program became one that we found a lot of live event potential, because they had a huge amount of listener interaction. They still do. They get many, many, many, many emails, tweets a week, according to what they've talked about on the show. They would come to us and say, "Hey, we're interested in doing a live show," and they would get hooked up with our executive director of planning and we would make that happen for them. The producer would come along, work with them, run the show, record it remotely and then put that out as a podcast as well. There's a lot of interaction between the hosts and the producers. But of course the hosts have the final sign-off on the shows.[35]

DON'T BE AFRAID TO DIG DEEP FOR CONTENT

Most of the podcasts discussed so far have been narrowly focused models addressing a single theme or topic. Generally, they're produced by a handful of people or maybe even just one individual. These models don't reflect all of podcasting. In fact, some podcasts, such as *Serial* and *This American Life*, can be quite complex in production and broad in the scope of topics they cover.

The weekly *Reveal* podcast, for example, which is produced by the Center for Investigative Reporting (CIR), is essentially the same content offered in the "Reveal" syndicated radio show, which is produced in partnership with the Public Radio Exchange (PRX). A typical 47-minute episode includes three segments, sometimes built around a single topic.

"Once in a while, however—I would say more frequently—we are adding some shorter pieces, and we may have as many as four or six," said Taki Telondis, CIR's senior radio editor.[36]

Sometimes, as in the episode covering the June 16, 2016, shooting at the Pulse nightclub in Orlando, Florida, the *Reveal* staff incorporates even more audio segments. Telondis says:

> I can't even remember how many pieces were in that, because we tried something entirely different: Having these little sort-of postcards and, [for] some of the victims, using sound from their social media pages and doing these little literally 45-second-to-1-minute-long little bits on these folks in that episode that probably had 9 or 10 elements.[37]

Producing this amount of content on a weekly basis requires more resources than most podcasters have access to.

"The CIR staff, the whole entire organization, is about 65 people," said Christa Scharfenberg, CIR's head of studio.

> Of that, 20 people are completely focused on the radio show and pod-cast. But all of our newsroom—another I think 25 people are investigative reporters who traditionally have worked more in text, editors; our data team and everybody—is contributing to the show in their own way. Some of those people are actually learning to produce radio.

More typically, they're working in partnership with a radio producer. I really feel like all 65 people, in one way or another, are contributing to the show, but 20 is the core radio production team.[38]

The *Reveal* staff develops content in a variety of ways, but usually the topic is grown "in-house" based on the investigation of a single reporter or group of reporters.

"Very often, one of the reporters will be looking into something and there's interest there. There's potential there," Telondis said, and the reporter will work with an editor to learn as much as possible.

What typically happens is this sort of pitch process that we've been developing: The reporter and the editor, when they think that they really have a story here that would work for *Reveal*, they fill out the pitch form for it. Once they do that, it enters this spreadsheet along with other pitches.[39]

Staff members, including radio editors, reporters and the executive producer, review the pitches and discuss them as a group.

That way anyone who has a comment or a question or a concern— whatever it may be, that is sort of aired to the group, and the reporter and editor answer those questions or concerns. It's a real open process, [a] very democratic process. After that, beyond that meeting for the whole staff, we will have a separate editorial discussion in which the decision will be made.[40]

Once a story has been green-lighted, a radio producer is assigned to it and a timeline is created.

The reporting clock starts ticking. If it's that type of story around which a particular theme can be developed into an entire episode, then we'll take that theme and try and populate the whole hour's worth of programming around it. Sometimes, we'll do call-outs to outside organizations, or we'll talk to our collaborators, or we'll just ask our own staff to start snooping around. "All right, we're interested in doing something on public defenders. Look for those kinds of stories." And then the thing just sort of builds, and there'll be an editor, like myself, assigned to that show.[41]

One of the things that makes *Reveal* different from many podcasts is that the staff will spend three or four months developing an episode.

"There's a lot going on at any given time, and editors, like Taki and his colleagues, are really involved, working with the reporters and producers all along on the script developments, the revisions, the editing," Scharfenberg said.

> It's a very labor-intensive process. Because of the sensitive nature of a lot of the reporting we do, everything gets lawyered at the end. There are investigative editors also looking at it. It's a very labor-intensive process compared to your typical sort of interview podcast.[42]

It's not unusual on the more professional or journalistic end of the podcasting spectrum, where a great deal of research, reporting and investigation needs to go into each segment, that producers juggle a number of different episodes in various stages of development.

When I interviewed Jessica Alpert, she had just posted the 23rd episode of the *Modern Love* podcast.

"I have about 43 on tape—not the back ends, only the front ends, and not mixed yet," she said. "We're going to do 48 this year."[43]

Alpert works with two other people to stay ahead of *Modern Love*'s weekly posting deadline. Each episode requires them to hire and record an actor to read the chosen essay from the New York Times' "Modern Love" database, record commentary by "Modern Love" editor Daniel Jones and track down and record an interview with the essay's writer. It's not just helpful but necessary to bank interviews or segments in advance, especially if the content takes time to produce. That reservoir of content provides a safety net in case something falls through.

> We just recorded an amazing essay that I really wanted to put on this week, and what's funny is we got the actor and that's all great. We got the mix started and then we found out that the essayist is in the wilderness and not near any phone or anything, so I guess we'll have to postpone that one. It is a lot of moving parts, and they all have to be coordinated.[44]

Alpert juggles "spreadsheet after spreadsheet after spreadsheet" to stay organized and keep track of all that content.

Despite these difficulties, Alpert has as a leg up on other podcasts when it comes to booking guests. With the exception of finding an actor to read the "Modern Love" essays, she already knows who she needs to talk to for a particular episode: Editor Jones and the essayist.[45]

BRING NEW VOICES INTO THE DISCUSSION

Unless you are the most articulate and fascinating host on the planet, you will want to have other voices on your podcast. The right guest can make a big splash. But identifying who you should talk to can be something of a challenge. You want to have someone who is an expert in the theme of your podcast or the topic of discussion for a particular episode. But he or she also needs to be someone who is "a good talker." Alpert said:

> I hear a lot of podcasts that book the most boring guests. They could be brilliant Harvard professors, but if their delivery is horrible you can't book them. You can't put them on a podcast. And I think you have to know when to, we used to call it, shoot your puppies. You know, when to kill the things that you may love but that just don't work. And it's hard sometimes, but you get much better at it. Maybe it's because I've worked on shows for so long that I'm able to know within probably the first 30 seconds whether someone will work or not, just by the way they speak.[46]

Aside from presenting a vocal variety that will be a more pleasant experience for your audience to listen to, other voices mean other perspectives. You want to avoid a podcast that's a droning lecture or a diatribe. Create a conversation instead. Delvac said:

> The thing that I really like about a good podcast is having diversity in the voices, said Julia Furlan, Buzzfeed podcast producer. The same way there is a texture in the rhythm, there's a texture in the sound of the voices and the kind of words they're using and the ways that they communicate. And I really like, for example, to hear a podcast that sounds very different. All of our podcasts have a very colloquial, very low-key or a sort of informal style that is clear, while also being very informal and conversational. I really love that about podcasts.[47]

Diversity of guests and even co-hosts is something that a lot of people probably don't think about enough when they're launching a podcast. You don't want to create a show in which two people from the same background who have the same perspective are agreeing all the time. You want an exchange of ideas that comes from a diversity of experiences.

"The democratization of media in all forms has been so powerful, especially for people whose voices tend to be marginalized by institutional power," Delvac said.[48]

Trust me. Even if the subject of your podcast is something you love and that you think you know inside and out, someone with another background and life experience is going to see it differently than you do.

Jennifer Crawford of *The JellyVision Show* organized the first DC PodFest in November 2015, where podcasters from the mid-Atlantic region shared their experiences. One of the more enlightening panels, entitled All Podcasters Are Not White, featured Jacksonrao of *The Nerdpocalypse* and Mary Nichols of *FuseBox Radio Broadcast*.

During the panel, Jacksonrao explained how *The Nerdpocalypse*'s African-American take on pop culture set it apart from the many other podcasts

FIGURE 3.4 Jay Jacksonrao is the host of *The Nerdpocalypse* podcast and the founder of the TNP Studios podcast network.

covering the same subjects. As an example, he explained how "The Flash," a superhero television show on the CW network, was really a story about the black family experience. After hero Barry Allen's mother is killed and his father imprisoned, a black detective and his daughter bring Barry into their family to live with them. Because the character was raised in an African-American household, that experience informs many of the decisions he makes throughout the series.

"I guess without going too deep into that, but shows like 'The Flash,' it's a very black show and it's secretly this black show, which is disguised as a superhero show," Jacksonrao said in an interview. "It's just kind of funny."[49]

As a lifelong comic-book reader and fan of "The Flash," I thought I knew everything about the show, but I didn't. It took someone with a different life experience and a similar love for the subject to show me something that I hadn't seen was there.

Find a person who understands the topic of your podcast, someone who is "a good talker" and who can teach you something new about the subject. Give them a voice, listen to their perspective, and share it with your audience. Delvac said:

> It's not just sort of exciting or—I hesitate to use the word—empowering. It's not just great that so many more people have access. It's also been really fun. It's really fun to get to do something that feels like absolutely whatever we want, in addition to being kind of professionally rewarding.[50]

ACTIVITIES

1. Plan out the topics for the first five episodes of your podcast. Who will be the host? Who are your guests? Try to come up with some regular segments for each episode as well as some features designed around the topic and guest of each particular episode. For example, if you have a radio deejay as a guest, why not ask what his or her desert-island music list is? Put as much detail into the plan as possible. Write out questions for each of your guests.

2. Make a production plan. How long will an episode be, and when will you be posting? Once you've figured that out, create a calendar for your production cycle, including pre-production (brainstorming topics, choosing guests, scheduling interviews); production (recording, editing audio and posting online); and post-production (promotion). As you begin to produce

and post episodes, production cycles for different shows will start to overlap. That's OK. It's important at this point to understand what work needs to be done for every episode and in what order. That will make it easier to divide the work and responsibilities.

3. What more can you be doing? This is something you always need to ask yourself, even before you've recorded that first episode. How are the topics and guests for this episode serving the bigger mission of the podcast? Am I finding good talkers? Will this be interesting to my audience, or will I be boring them? Write down what the goal of the podcast is and how this episode serves the overarching mission. Write down a new question, segment or approach that might make this episode better.

NOTES

1 Mackey, Phil (2016, Sept. 13). Personal interview.
2 Delvac, Gina (2016, July 11). Phone interview.
3 Ibid.
4 Ibid.
5 Ibid.
6 Ibid.
7 Ibid.
8 Crawford, Jennifer and Timothy Trueheart (2016, June 6). Personal interview.
9 Ibid.
10 Ibid.
11 Poor, Nigel (2016, July 7). Personal interview.
12 Ibid.
13 Ibid.
14 Ibid.
15 Ibid.
16 Ibid.
17 Noorbakhsh, Zahra (2016, June 28). Phone interview.
18 Ibid.
19 Ibid.
20 Ibid.
21 Ibid.
22 Coulter, Dave and Kat Jessup (2016, May 13). Personal interview.
23 Ibid.
24 Ibid.
25 Jacksonrao, Jay (2016, June 13). Skype interview.
26 Ibid.
27 Ibid.
28 Ibid.
29 Ibid.
30 Mayer, Laura (2016, June 8). Phone interview.

31 Ibid.
32 Ibid.
33 Ibid.
34 Ibid.
35 Ibid.
36 Scharfenberg, Christa and Taki Telondis (2016, June 24). Phone interview.
37 Ibid.
38 Ibid.
39 Ibid.
40 Ibid.
41 Ibid.
42 Ibid.
43 Alpert, Jessica (2016, June 17). Phone interview.
44 Ibid.
45 Ibid.
46 Ibid.
47 Furlan, Julia (2016, June 10). Phone interview.
48 Delvac.
49 Jacksonrao.
50 Delvac.

4

Turn Your Ideas into Audio

At its core, a podcast exists in two states; one conceptual, one physical. Up to this point, we've focused mainly on the conceptual side of the equation: What is my podcast going to be about? Who is my audience? What will it sound like? Answering all of these questions defines the core of a podcast, that thing you will be marketing to others and, hopefully, building on week to week, or month to month, or whatever the frequency of your podcast is. It's your content.

Although your podcast may spring from the conceptual realm of ideas, it also has a physical side. Launching a podcast requires you to create an audio file, an MP3, which you'll post online. That file is the delivery system for your content, the object your audience downloads to access your ideas.

Chapter 2 described how to set up a studio and what recording equipment you'll need, thereby establishing an environment to create an MP3 file. This chapter will deal with the recording process, how you'll gather the pieces of audio necessary to make a podcast episode. Chapter 6 will discuss how to bring all those pieces together through the editing process.

AUTHENTICITY IS THE COIN OF THE REALM

A familial love of good storytelling is what inspired Bill McKenna to start the interrogatively named *Not Another Podcast?*

My mother and my father had a newspaper shop where I grew up in Dunellen, New Jersey, a small town. My dad would tell stories. He was basically the unofficial town historian. He always told great stories, whether he was in college or something else. As an homage to my mother and father who had passed away, I'd been told I could tell some pretty good stories too. It was just originally an outlet for me to deal with my mother and father's passing. But as time got on, it's become something more than that.[1]

Prior to launching his podcast in June 2014, McKenna had worked at a WVWC, a small radio station at West Virginia Wesleyan College. "I didn't do any technical things at all," he said. "I would just show up and speak into a microphone."[2]

McKenna's podcasting co-host, Brett Simons, did some radio in college at Shepherd University and worked in radio in West Virginia for a few years, where he did audio production. But McKenna does all the production on their podcast now.

The two met when McKenna moved to the Washington, DC, suburb of Herndon, Virginia, in 2009.

We became friends at Jimmy's Old Town Tavern playing trivia. His wealth of knowledge, just an array of knowing pop culture, sports and things of that nature, and my similarities in that, I thought . . . he was going to be a guest on the first episode of my show. He was there. The first show went really well, and then five shows into it, he was still there, so I was like, "Do you want to do this full time with me?" So that's where it kind of evolved.[3]

Not Another Podcast? is a tongue-in-cheek examination of suburban life, with discussions ranging across sports, commuting, professional wrestling and the 9-to-5 daily grind. But it's the duo's forays into the personal aspects of their lives that generate the greatest response. McKenna said:

When Prince passed away, Brett intimated on the show that when he was younger he wore a Prince shirt when he was in eighth grade and he got ridiculed for it because Prince was different. He felt terrible about it. He's older now, but he got really upset when the same people who ridiculed him were posting on Facebook how sad it was. It really

FIGURE 4.1 Bill McKenna hosts *Not Another Podcast?* out of his home studio.

hurt him to the core. He said, "I know this shouldn't be affecting me now, but it does."[4]

Simons' admission triggered an outpouring of support from the podcast's listeners.

I can't tell you how many people responded. I let Brett know. I took screenshots, and people were sending me texts and emails. I was like, "Brett, just so you know, you did a great thing." He was really worried about it at first. He was like, "I don't know if I should've talked about it." I was like: "Are you kidding me? That's what people want. They want a sincere emotion. You weren't being condescending, and you weren't being mean. You were being the 12-year-old Brett as opposed to the 44-year-old Brett. That resonated with a lot of people."[5]

What "clicked" with McKenna and Simons' listeners was their sincerity, a rare commodity in the world of mass media. But it's an element that podcasting is well-suited to deliver.

Listeners have an intimate relationship with a podcast. A podcaster's voice is in listeners' earbuds. You're their lone companion as they drive to work or exercise at the gym. They recognize when you're being sincere, and they respond when you're authentic. You're not a huckster trying to sell them something. You're their friend.

"You can hear sincerity in someone's voice," McKenna said. "It's interesting."[6]

Authenticity is the coin of the realm in the podcasting world, so you should strive to create content that your audience will perceive is authentic.

A mistake that many people make when they start a conversation-based podcast like *Not Another Podcast?* is thinking it's just a matter of turning on the microphones and then the "magic happens." Unless you've got a background in improvisational theater, that's not going to happen. Even improv starts out with a premise, a foundation on which to build.

Another way to look at it is you're creating a new experience for your audience, but you're presenting it in a familiar way. Think of poets or songwriters: They come up with the words and ideas they wish to express and then present them to an audience through the conventions of their artistic expression, such as a sonnet or a love song.

The object of recording a podcast is to create something "authentic," but to do that, you need to create a thing that is somewhat artificial. You want your podcast to have a beginning, a middle and an end, not just a random recording of two people talking.

Although McKenna and Simons don't work off of scripts, they work off of a structure. They create storyboards for each recording session, which contain a list of news topics that they plan to discuss. Each episode begins with a "housekeeping" segment, in which they thank listeners and talk about what they'll be discussing. They also encourage listeners to visit amazon. com and use the podcast's promotional code to purchase items; this helps finance the show.

When all the housekeeping is done, the podcast begins in earnest, with a discussion about what McKenna and Simons did on their weekend and what they'll be doing in the coming week. The "magic" occurs within the framework they constructed.

> I think me and Brett could go at least three hours, to be honest with you. We scale it down so that our listeners can listen to it in 20-to-30-minute chunks at a time or listen to the whole thing. We've actually thought about doing two 30-minute segments, one being for news and pop culture and one specifically for sports. But we haven't gotten there yet. But I think that's where it's ending up going.[7]

START OUT WITH A PLAN OF ATTACK

When you sit down to record your first podcast, you need a structure in place to guide what you're going to record. It can be a storyboard, like the one McKenna and Simons use, or a list of questions you want to ask your guest.

All of the photographers or videographers I've interviewed on *It's All Journalism* follow the same procedure when they get an assignment. They identify the people they need to get photos of, investigate the location where they'll be shooting, and then they'll create a shot list. This is exactly what it sounds like: A list of the different types of photos they want to get so they can tell a story when they get back to the newsroom.

If a photographer is covering a parade, for example, she'll want to get photos of the bands, beauty queens and floats, as well as reaction shots of the crowd. She'll need photos of children and families. Then, she'll look for unusual angles. Maybe she can climb up on a fire engine or hang out of a second-story window to take photos of the parade route. All the while, the photographer is assembling a variety of content to inform the story she will be telling.

Tiffany Campbell, the executive editor for digital at WBUR in Boston, got her start producing multimedia stories for the Seattle Times.

> For me, I was never working alone. I was often working with a photographer and a print reporter. In that scenario, there's even more pressure, along with the source, to make sure that you're not holding anybody up, you're not interfering with anybody else, that they don't have to wait for you to mess around with your equipment. All of which kind of happened a couple of times. That really solidified for me that, when you're doing stuff like this, it's so much different from print reporting because, as opposed to just needing your notebook, you really need to have that baseline set and organized.[8]

Putting together a "shot list" before you start recording a podcast is not a bad approach. Campbell said this can help you get a sense beforehand of what you need to get to make sense of the story.

GET TO KNOW YOUR GUESTS AHEAD OF TIME

With all this talk of planning before recording, I don't want to give the impression that spontaneity is a bad thing. You want to be able to go where the conversation takes you. But you also want to be an informed host. Think of yourself as the bus driver of your podcast. You want to have an idea where you're headed, while avoiding dead ends or driving off a cliff.

Dead ends and cliff dives are real hazards for podcasters, especially when you add a guest into the mix. Not only do you want to be prepared to create a great episode, but, more importantly, you want to be prepared for your guests' sakes. They've taken time out of their busy schedules to appear on your podcast. Don't waste their time with a lack of preparation. Even if your podcast is a hobby, be professional.

Joey Kissimmee is the founder of Appendipity, a company that designs WordPress themes for podcasting websites. He also interviews fellow entrepreneurs on his podcast, *Income Press*. Do you know what Kissimmee hates? People who don't prepare for interviews.

> I heard a podcast the other day of a guy—I'm not going to name—
> but a guy giving tips on [interviewing], and he said "Just don't do
> research; just do it on the fly." Come on, are you serious? That's the
> worst advice you could give someone. Do your research on those
> people.[9]

As an example, he cited how doing research helped him get a great interview with Natalie Sisson, host of *The Suitcase Entrepreneur*.

> I would have never known that she was a bodybuilder, a body sculpt
> artist. I would have never known these little things about people like
> that. And when I brought that to her attention, she was like, "Wow,
> nobody's ever asked me that!"[10]

Once he's done his research, Kissimmee writes everything in bullet points,
but he doesn't stick to any particular order during the interview.

> Probably the only things that are in order are the first three ques-
> tions, because after those, one of those is going to segue into a con-
> versation. That's key, segue. That's another art form you have to learn,
> how to segue. I hear this a lot. I could tell a podcast show when it's
> really scripted, because they don't know how to segue into another
> question. They just follow the bullet points in order. Man, sometimes,
> people give me nothing and converse, but whatever they tell me, it
> segues. Maybe if I'm in bullet point number 3 it'll segue to bullet point
> number 10.[11]

Kissimmee sends his guests the bullet points only if they ask for them in
advance. In those cases, he may send them just five bullet points, so they have
a rough idea what the conversation is going to be about. Of course, most of the
people Kissimmee is talking to—entrepreneurs like Sisson, John Lee Dumas of
EOFire, Pat Flynn of *The Smart Passive Income Blog* and Andrew Warner of
Mixergy—are experienced podcast guests and know how to carry a conversation.

> When they get interviewed, they're getting asked the same questions.
> And it's a breath of fresh air to them when it's really off the cuff and
> you're just rolling with the flow. So . . . the top three questions . . .
> I actually do keep in order, and I let that segue into a conversation.
> And, like with Natalie Sisson, pretty much all that interview after that

FIGURE 4.2 Here, a podcaster is running his microphones through a mixer so he can adjust the sound levels before they're recorded on his digital recorder. With this setup, he could hook up additional microphones to interview more guests. He could also run a cable from the mixer through an audio interface and into the USB port of a laptop or desktop computer.

first question, it was all just off the cuff and segued right from the conversation. It was a true conversation.[12]

It's All Journalism is an interview-based podcast, and we follow a nearly identical procedure for every interview we do. After booking a guest, I'll write up a set of questions and send them to the guest a couple of days before the recording. [See Appendix C.]

The reason for doing this is twofold. First, I want guests to feel comfortable about the interview, to feel that I'm not looking to sandbag them with any "gotcha" questions—we don't do that type of podcast. Second, it gives guests some time to prepare. That way, when I ask the questions, they won't be surprised and fumble for an answer. They'll present the information clearly and in a way that's informative and enjoyable to listen to.

But if they know what I'm going to ask, where's the spontaneity? Where's the surprise? Where's the authenticity of a true conversation?

Remember, a podcast is an artificial construct. The questions are the framework I'm using to guide that "conversation" and create an experience for the listener that has a beginning, a middle and an end. I'm building it as I go along, based upon a plan. The questions get me where I'm going.

For our podcast, I take a journalist's approach. I ask questions, listen to answers and then ask more questions based on what the guest says. Within that framework, I can be very loose and open to the flow of our conversation. More often than not, I'll get the ball rolling by asking only one or two of the questions I sent the guest; after that, we go where the conversation takes us. I may wrap things up by asking a question that ties everything together. If everything goes as planned, I'll have a podcast that's structured but conversational, one that sounds spontaneous but is really very guided in how it's put together.

This style of interviewing was adapted from how interviews are done at the place where I work. Unlike a podcast, which can go on as long as it needs to, interviews at Federal News Radio must be recorded to precise lengths of time in order to fit around the commercials, newscasts and other elements of a live radio show. Interview segments generally run 5–10 minutes. Interviewers and guests need to know exactly what they're going to say in that limited time. That's why all the guests receive questions ahead of time and the hosts work off of a script. Thought needs to go into these elements ahead of time so that the audience will get the full news story from the interview.

It should be noted that for much of the journalism world, sending a guest the questions beforehand is not a standard practice.

"No, never give them questions ever," said Jessica Alpert, managing producer for program development at WBUR and a member of the *Modern Love* podcast production team. "We don't do that at all."[13]

There are good reasons for this choice as well.

"If you were doing an investigative report and you're sitting down with your prime source, you don't want this person to have a bunch of time to prepare their rebuttals on why they're innocent," said Campbell of WBUR.

> But at the same time, you want to give people a fair shake too. It's pretty common, no matter what you're doing. You wouldn't just

call someone up and say, "I'm not revealing anything I'm [going to be] talking about. I'm just going to show up." You're still having that conversation.[14]

There's nothing wrong with telling your interviewee, in broad terms, what you want to talk about. Or not. Politicians and other public officials, for example, are used to answering questions on the fly, so journalists tend to not provide them with questions ahead of time. But in those situations, you should always be prepared to not get an answer to your question.

Another approach is to conduct a pre-interview of the guest. Sometimes the show's producer will do an unrecorded pre-interview, and the host will record his or her own interview with the guest as the podcast.

Although Alpert said she wouldn't send guests questions ahead of time, she didn't seem to think pre-interviewing was inherently bad or good. It can be time consuming, but it might give you a sense of whether the person you're talking to would be a good guest.

> If you can do a pre-interview with someone, take advantage. Not only will you be prepared, you may have asked a lot of these people who you do pre-interviews with, they'll come to the table and say, "You know, I was thinking a lot about that question you asked. And you know, this is what I want to say about that." So sometimes it's really helpful. Now, if you're talking to a newsmaker who may change their mind about talking to you, don't do a pre-interview. Just get them on tape.[15]

For an episode of *Modern Love*, the producers typically pre-interview the essayist in order to see how his or her life has changed since The New York Times published the essay.

> It's just finding out what's happened since. What was the reaction to the essay? What's life like now? Maybe if there were some unanswered questions [in the piece]. Obviously, anything you would want to know. We go there during the pre-interview and then we go there again when they're on tape or we go even deeper. With some of the more painful stories, the pre-interview is also time for us to establish some sort of rapport with the essayist and also figure out if they don't want to go somewhere, what those boundaries may be.[16]

Like Alpert, Laura Mayer, the managing producer at Panoply, has roots in public broadcasting. She was an associate producer of "On the Media" and "Fishko Files" at WNYC in New York.

> When I was at "On the Media," so much of the producer's work was pre-interviewing. The way that was able to be done without messing up the conversation with the host is a host wasn't doing the pre-interviewing, the producer was. It felt like a fresh conversation when it was actually being recorded.[17]

Despite seeing this practice at work at her old job, Mayer said pre-interviewing is not something Panoply typically does for its podcasts.

"I think there could be some exceptions," she said. "Sometimes a celebrity will have a team that requires it, and maybe that will happen, but I think that's very, very rare."[18]

The idea of not pre-interviewing comes from Mayer's experience as a podcast listener and as the person who manages Panoply's various podcasts.

> The big thing with *Slate* and Panoply, with the chat shows, is we're really trying to keep up the spontaneity of a normal human-to-human conversation. I think a lot of the pre-interviewing and providing questions ahead of time can kind of leave a lot of good stuff in the locker room, or whatever that phrase is. If the host and the guest know that this is what the questions are going to be, then everybody has kind of prepared to have this preordained conversation. What we're really trying to get at, with these chat shows especially, is just the idea of a listener being able to drop in and hear intelligent people have a natural conversation.[19]

Although Mayer prefers not to pre-interview, that doesn't mean the producers of Panoply's podcasts don't prepare for each episode.

> For the chat shows, they have prep. The producers will provide prep for them. I would say it's nowhere near like the kind of prep work you would do, for example, with the Malcolm Gladwell [host of *Revisionist History*] show. There's a lot of prep for that. If he knew he was trying to get a specific story out of them, Malcolm would work with the producer to kind of figure out, "OK, what do you want to hit that

with?" That kind of process is more similar to the NPR model. We still do prep and background research, but it's less intensive than what I was doing at WNYC.[20]

Another approach with prepping that some radio producers use is explaining to guests ahead of time how they should frame their answers. Typically, they'll want guests to repeat the question as part of their answer. For example, if you ask someone, "Where did you grow up?" the guest would reply, "I grew up in Chicago" rather than just "Chicago."

This approach is commonly used by a reporter who is weaving together multiple pieces of audio with voiceover narration. In this scenario, each audio interview needs to stand as a self-contained element. The narrative tells the larger story that the interview elements illustrate. By having the guest begin an answer by repeating the question, it frees up the reporter so he doesn't have to ask a question in the narrative. Here's an example:

> *Narration*: "Mary Johnson saw her first skyscraper when she was a child."

> *Interview*: "I grew up in Chicago, after my parents moved from the country."

I can imagine advocates of pure, spontaneous conversation shuddering at the thought of this kind of manipulation of an interview subject. It's not something I've ever done, nor would it be something I'd advocate for a typical conversation-based podcast. But this approach can be useful with a certain type of audio storytelling, where you're trying to blend multiple elements into a smooth narrative. You're not asking the person to lie. You're asking them to give you the same information, but in a way that can help you tell the story better.

BE CURIOUS, ASK QUESTIONS AND LISTEN

One of the great pleasures of being a journalist is getting the opportunity to train new reporters or interns. Interns are especially fun, because many of them have little to no experience working in a newsroom.

When I was a newspaper editor, one of the first things I'd do with the interns is send them out on man-on-the-street interviews. It's really the big test. If you can't go up to a perfect stranger, ask them their name, where they live and a question, you're going to have a tough time being a reporter.

It's unfair of me to say that doing an interview is easy, because I've been doing them most of my life. But truthfully, doing a good interview is just being curious, asking the right questions and listening.

"I think the most important thing about interviewing is to ask simple questions and listen," said Steve Nelson, formerly director of on-demand programming for American Public Media and now director of programming at NPR.

> That's my big advice for people, if I can put it in a nutshell. You have to do your prep, you have to kind of know what you want to ask. You don't want to walk into an interview and sit down with a list of questions and then just read the list of questions. That's a terrible way to interview. You want to listen. Find what's interesting.[21]

Ask questions that draw people out, Nelson said, and keep your questions simple.

> You're going to get a much better answer to saying something like, "Why did you feel that way?" or "How did that make you feel?" than listing, "Oh, did you feel happy or sad or what?" . . . Keep it simple and then listen to what the person says. Let them guide the story in the way that they're thinking about it rather than how you're thinking about it.[22]

According to Alpert, the key to conducting a good interview is to be a curious person and just be yourself.

> I really think it's just about curiosity and listening to people. Listen to people who do interviews, and watch how they go deep. Listen to how they go deep. That's key. There's a ton of really good people who are amazing interviewers. There's tons of different styles out there. But I really do think you learn by listening, and you learn just by doing.[23]

IT'S TIME TO RECORD YOUR FIRST EPISODE

It's 9 p.m. on a Wednesday and you're sitting in your dining room, which is the quietest room in your apartment. For your first episode, you've decided to keep it simple and interview a friend about a movie you both know really well. You love the film. He hates it.

In front of each of you sits a dynamic microphone affixed to a metal stand. From the bottom of each microphone, an XLR cable loops to the center of the table and plugs into one of the inputs of a four-track, HD4 Zoom digital recorder. You double-check the connection to make sure the cables click in place.

Now, you each don a pair of headphones that completely cover your ears. Complete silence. One of you pushes the record button on the recorder, which has a two-step recording setup. If you click it once, you can check your levels. Click it a second time and the recording will start.

With just one click, you can hear your voice fine. Your friend says something, but you can't hear him.

First you check the headphone volume. That's up to the highest setting. Then you notice his microphone is switched off. Once he turns it on, his voice comes in loud and clear.

Looking at the display on the recorder, you watch the audio levels as you each take turns speaking into your microphones. Your friend is sitting a little too far away from the microphone. You need to get in really close, about three inches from the foam microphone cover. He slides his chair up.

"Testing. Testing. One—two—three. This is me talking into a microphone."

The audio bars go to the middle of the display. The sound looks good. You adjust the volume on your headphones so you can hear each other.

All your prep is behind you. You've thought about the theme of your podcast and come up with a topic for the first episode. You looked up everything you could about the movie you're going to discuss and even made a list of trivia to share. When your friend showed up, he told you he'd written a quiz about the lead actor as something to discuss.

The last thing you do is jot down an introduction with the things you want to say at the start: Who you both are, the name of the podcast, what it's about and the topic for tonight's recording.

You push the record button a second time, and the clock begins to count. Now the fun starts.

ONE LAST THING...

When it's over, you turn off the recorder and laugh a little bit. Your first podcast is in the can.

Not quite. The work's not done until you've checked what you just recorded.

Pick up the recorder and play back part of the audio to make sure it sounds OK. Skip ahead several times to make sure the audio quality is good throughout. If you want, remove the SD card from your digital recorder and insert it in your computer. Open your audio editing program and import the file. If the audio wave looks all right and sounds good when you play it back, you're done for the night. You and your friend can have a beer.

You'll still need to edit and post the audio, but the first big step is done. Congratulations.

ACTIVITIES

1. Create a storyboard for your first episode. Write out a script for each segment (introduction, games, quiz, outro, etc.). Familiarize yourself with your guests' biographies and come up with questions that elicit a response, such as "What did it feel like when you quit your dream job?" If possible, pre-interview your guest. Also, listen to or read other interviews to make sure you're not asking questions that your guest may have heard a thousand times before.

2. Hook up all of your equipment and play around a bit. Familiarize yourself with the settings of your digital recorder, computer, smartphone or tablet. Read the technical manuals. Record 30-second segments with each of your microphones, identifying how they need to be positioned to get the best sound. Go ahead and set up your studio as if you were recording an episode. As you listen back to test recordings, identify any ambient noise that needs to be eliminated from the studio space.

3. Conduct a dry run before you record the first episode. Record a 5-to-10-minute podcast in which you interview a friend. This will give you

a chance to test out your equipment and become more comfortable with the idea of podcasting. After you're done, listen back to the audio and give yourself a critical review. Did you sound nervous? Was the audio quality OK? Did it seem boring? Be tough on yourself. Ask a friend whose judgment you trust to give it a listen. You're not looking for praise. You want an honest review from which you can learn and improve.

NOTES

1 McKenna, Bill (2016, May 17). Phone interview.
2 Ibid.
3 Ibid.
4 Ibid.
5 Ibid.
6 Ibid.
7 Ibid.
8 Thompson, Caitlin (2016, June 15). Phone interview.
9 Kissimmee, Joey (2016, June 16). Phone interview.
10 Ibid.
11 Ibid.
12 Ibid.
13 Alpert, Jessica (2016, June 17). Phone interview.
14 Campbell, Tiffany (2016, May 21). Skype interview.
15 Alpert.
16 Ibid.
17 Mayer, Laura (2016, June 8). Phone interview.
18 Ibid.
19 Ibid.
20 Ibid.
21 Nelson, Steve (2016, June 2). Phone interview.
22 Ibid.
23 Alpert.

5

Bring the World into Your Podcast

For many people, the idea of a podcast is just two guys sitting in a garage talking about comic books. It's a useful cliché. It conjures up an image of a pair of amateur broadcasters so passionate about a subject that they've separated themselves from the rest of the world and are talking into microphones to an invisible audience of who knows how many strangers online.

The characterization is a little dismissive, to be sure. A lot of us take comfort that we're at least recording our podcasts in the living room and not the garage. But where you record neither validates your passion nor defines the scope of your podcast. In fact, with the portable recording technology available today, you can pretty much record anywhere.

One of the goals discussed earlier in this book is to create a recording space where you'll feel comfortable learning how to podcast. It's important that early on you master your equipment and understand what makes good sounding audio free of outside interference.

As your podcast grows, maybe you'll dedicate a room to recording, buy better microphones and put up sound-proofing materials. In a sense, you'll be building a more permanent studio. That's great. Just make sure you're not building yourself an inescapable cocoon.

Back in Chapter 2, I relayed our experience trying to record at the 2014 Online News Association conference in Chicago. The lesson learned from that fiasco was that our podcast was tethered to the studio and if we wanted to go out in the field, we had to learn how to be more mobile.

As a result of that lesson, we could've accepted that *It's All Journalism* was simply a studio-bound podcast and any out-of-town guests would be interviewed remotely by Skype or other means. Plenty of podcasts are successful using that model.

But, being able to go out to a location occasionally and conduct an interview outside a studio is both an enriching experience and an opportunity to incorporate natural sound into your show.

Out of the blue, a friend invited me to cover the Society for News Design's 2015 workshop in Washington, DC, for *It's All Journalism*. I didn't do any planning. I tossed my Zoom H4n digital recorder, a couple of dynamic microphones, some XLR cables, my laptop, two pairs of headphones and extra batteries and SD cards into a backpack.

At the conference, I scoped out a few presentations and asked some of the speakers afterward if they could spare 15 minutes for a quick interview. We'd find a quiet corner, I'd give them a microphone to hold and a pair of headphones to wear, and I'd turn on the recorder. After a quick intro, I just asked five or six questions off the top of my head based on what I'd heard during the presentation.

The interviews were short—I think the longest was 20 minutes—but they were fun, informative and entertaining. When I finished producing them, they all sounded much more lively and spontaneous than our studio-bound podcasts. It was a great learning experience, and I felt much more confident about going out and doing a podcast live.

Since then, I've had several opportunities to go out in the field. My favorite moment came at the 2015 Association of Alternative Newsmedia conference in Salt Lake City. I got a chance to interview a former MTV veejay, who was speaking about his new online music venture.

After he gave his presentation, we moved to the conference hotel's cafe for a one-on-one interview. The recording had been going for about 10 minutes, and we were in the middle of a pleasant conversation, when the cafe had a sudden rush on lattes. For a good five minutes, we tried speaking over a very loud cappuccino machine as it belched out cup after cup of steamed foam.

My guest laughed about it as we talked. His background was in radio and television, so he suggested that I could edit this section of the interview out. I responded that this was podcasting, not professional radio. The coffee-maker provided good natural sound.

Editing the episode later, I decided to keep the section with the noisy cappuccino machine intact. It added something to the interview. It was real. Our reactions were real. It gave an authentic sense of place to our conversation, something we could never reproduce in the studio.

Since there was no danger of me starting the *Noisy Cappuccino Machine* podcast, I thought the few minutes of intrusive sound would not overburden the listener. They'd hear our reactions and understand the humor of the moment and share it with us. They'd appreciate the experience more.

Tiffany Campbell, the executive editor for digital at WBUR in Boston, is a big advocate of weaving natural sound into a podcast to give texture to a story. When she was producing multimedia stories for The Seattle Times, she had many opportunities to go out in the field and to work on sound-based stories.

"The most important things to get are the interviews, but they are really challenging in the field because you're interviewing somebody in the middle of a barn," she said, as an example.

> That's a crazy, very noisy place. That can be part of the story, and that kind of lends itself . . . to actually bringing people into that story. Interviewing them there is good. It's good to get that, but there's a happy medium between making sure you've got that mic really well placed, really tight up there for them. You've got them mic'd so that it's really just background noise that kind of lends itself to the sense of place as opposed to the screaming-and-not-being-able-to-hear-them kind of situation.[1]

On one assignment, Campbell and a photographer spent 24 hours at Seattle's Pike Place Market gathering images and sound.

That was so much fun, because there was so much different stuff to do, [recording] everything from the birds cooing to the garbage pickup to the fruit being dumped in baskets to the people talking. You start to listen in a totally different way when you're approaching production like that. . . . You've got to get out there and walk around for a bit and actually be in the location for a second to try to figure out what you're trying to target. It does depend on the story. The 24 hours in Pike Place was an ambient, what-does-it-sound-like situation, so that was really wide-ranging and that was really fun.[2]

Just like a good interview, gathering quality ambient sound requires you to use your ears to envision the story.

Campbell stressed the importance of "listening for a while and having your headphones on—always have your headphones on—and just kind of absorbing it for a little while and then start to try and isolate things. You're trying to get one great minute of the busker on the corner, and you're just going to do that. You're just going to be able to take things in steps and not just holding your mic up in the air."[3]

Another time, Campbell was at a large fair in Washington state, covering a food story.

The reporter was leading the way, because she was choosing which booths we were going to and things like that. Even when you got up to it, it was interesting to listen, like, "What does it sound like when the chicken is on the grill?" or "What does it sound like when the corn dog is being fried?" or "What does the machine sound like that's making cotton candy?"[4]

Gather a variety of sounds to tell a big story.

WTOP radio reporter Neal Augenstein had never really listened to a podcast before CBS producer Mike Vele asked him whether he wanted to produce one about the Hannah Graham murder investigation for the "48 Hours" television series.

Augenstein had covered the Graham case ever since the University of Virginia student first went missing on Sept. 13, 2014. He followed the entire investigation, as the Charlottesville, Virginia, community first searched for the missing female student, then, after her body was found, mourned her loss.

Once police apprehended suspect Jesse Matthew, Augenstein reported on the trial and Matthew's eventual conviction. He knew the story inside and out.

CBS's offer came shortly after *Serial* had made a big splash with its episode-by-episode reporting of the Hae Min Lee murder investigation. Augenstein listened to *Serial* to try to get a sense of what producing a podcast might actually mean.

FIGURE 5.1 Neal Augenstein is a reporter for WTOP radio in Washington, DC. He produced *The Hannah Graham Story* podcast for CBS's "48 Hours."

"I liked the flow. It was sort of an old radio drama mixed with long-form audio that I would do at WTOP," Augenstein said.

> I could certainly see there were enough elements of the Hannah Graham story that we could generate a podcast. When I spoke with Mike, though, it was clear that neither of us had any idea what this podcast would be about, what the format would be. Would it be chronological? Would it be different elements or little snippets of interesting moments? Other than period of time, that's sort of where things came together.[5]

CBS gave Augenstein complete freedom to structure the podcast in any way he thought best.

> I sort of came up with something that was largely chronological. But I was also thinking about the audio that I already had, thinking what little moments I could magnify. What juicy moments or juicy exchanges could I do more storytelling [with] than just relaying what happened.[6]

Augenstein had plenty of experience in his 20 years at WTOP producing long-form audio pieces. Listening to *Serial*, he recalled similar stories he'd done that involved the use of natural sound.

> I was thinking of it in terms of what I was familiar with. Radio pieces at WTOP, at least, involve a lot of natural sound. They involve a lot of letting the other person, the newsmaker, do the talking. As I listened to *Serial*, I noticed that there was next to no natural sound in it. It was usually, like a lot of things that NPR does, somebody sounding really nice in a studio, but they weren't using the natural sound to help paint the picture of what was happening. I envisioned that I would like to use a lot more natural sound to help paint the picture. That's something I do in my radio reports, so I knew at some point that I was going to integrate natural sound into the podcast.[7]

The first thing he did was review all the tape he'd gathered in covering the case, as well as audio recorded by other WTOP reporters. He was looking for elements that could tell different aspects of the story.

> For instance, there was a prayer or rally or candlelight vigil in which not only people were speaking at the podium, but there was also a

choir singing, and there was also organ music that was played. In the same way that I do for a radio piece, I set that aside and I wrote it down in my log of audio bits that I had. I knew that when it came to the point of telling about this vigil, I had a nice two-minute organ instrumental piece that I could use in putting the thing together.[8]

A colleague had recorded the sound of the police going through then-suspect Matthew's apartment.

When police were going through his home, [WTOP reporter] Mike Murillo shot YouTube video as the police were coming out. So not only did we have the police chief talking at the podium, but there was also the sound of the officers walking out, reporters calling out for them, them not saying anything. You heard them opening a car door, dropping these cardboard boxes into the van, slamming the door shut and starting the car and driving away. That natural sound segment was very helpful in describing the search of that day. I think that really helped bring people to the scene better than just telling them about what happened.[9]

Augenstein thinks a lot about ambient sound when he's driving to a story. He tries to imagine what he could record that would help illustrate the piece he's reporting on.

I think of it in terms of two different kinds of sounds. I think of it in terms of ambient sound, which is just standing in the middle of a room, holding the microphone up in the air and try[ing] to get the general hubbub of the sound that is going on. That is often used when it's my voice; later on when I go and I track my piece and I look for some unobtrusive but present sound, I'll use that ambient sound.[10]

Whenever Augenstein interviews someone, he'll also record at least a minute of natural sound in the same location, with no one around speaking or making any noise. When he's back in the studio editing, he'll use that as a sound bed for his own narration. "That way, when I mix that person's voice with my voice, it sounds like we're standing in the same place," he said.

Augenstein also records what he calls "identifiable sound."

If I were at a stakeout, [like] where they were searching Jesse Matthew's home, I would try to put my microphone right nearby as the officers were unrolling the crime scene tape, because that would make a sound that people would be able to identify without having the reporter say, "That's the sound of police tape being unrolled." You sort of think about what kind of identifiable sounds can a person listen to and immediately know the location where they are without the reporter having to describe what they're listening to.[11]

Identifiable sound can be very effective in transitioning between scenes in a story.

If we're changing locations or changing parts of the story, then the transitional natural sound will be used, followed by a different sound, by a different ambient bed. For instance, if you're out at a parade, let's say you wanted to transition from having the sound of the marching band, then you get up close to a sousaphone and you get the "Boomp, boomp, boomp, boomp." Then you would cut to the next scene. Let's say that it was a library. So you just hear the quiet sound of a person's footsteps walking down a hollow hallway. You let that establish for a few seconds. You let the audience catch up with you and almost anticipate. You want the audience to be able to follow along and to say: "Oh yeah, I hear they've changed places. Where are they? OK, they're in a library."[12]

The key to making this work is to keep the transition at a slow enough pace so that the audience can follow along before you introduce another new sound, such as narration. Listeners don't have visual cues telling them the scene has changed. You have to give the listener's brain a few seconds to understand that you're reporting on a new location.

Once you gather all the sounds, it's almost like an artist with a palette, thinking: "I'll use a little bit of orange here. I'll use a little gray as the background." But now I want to do something dramatic here, so I'll drop in some identifiable sound and then the listener will know that we're doing a transition in the story.[13]

Even though Augenstein already had a lot of material to draw from, he knew he was going to need more to inform all five episodes of *The Hannah Graham Story*.

"I'd already mapped out the entire series," he said. "I already had the script for the entire series, but I needed natural sound to do some transitions."[14]

Augenstein made a special trip to Charlottesville and to the campus of the University of Virginia, where he gathered natural sound. While there, he also recorded voice tracks at some of the locations involved in the story. Before he left for Charlottesville, though, he had a list of places to visit, sounds to record and passages from his script that he needed to do voice-over for.

> I knew that I needed to go right on the grounds there and record the sound of the church bell. I made sure I was there at the top of the hour to make sure I could get the sound of the church bell ringing. I wasn't speaking, I was just recording the natural sound. If I tried to record it live while the church bell was ringing, if I'd messed it up, I'd have to wait for another hour. I just recorded the natural sound and I checked it off my list.[15]

Several moments in his story took place at the downtown mall in Charlottesville, an open, outdoor expanse of restaurants, shops and music venues that Graham visited the night she disappeared.

> I wanted to get a whole bunch of ambient sound there. I had somebody playing a steel drum that happened to be on the mall. I made sure that I got up close when someone was at one of the outdoor restaurants, so I could get the clinks of silverware on plates as people were eating outside.[16]

Standing outside an open-air club, Augenstein held up his microphone and recorded the sound of a nightclub. Then he walked down the mall, holding the microphone down by his feet so he could get the sound of footsteps.

> Those are little tricks that most reporters will do. There are going to be times where you're going to be leafing through something, so you'll pretty dramatically record the sound of flipping pages—one of the most identifiable sounds that you can use. When there were people holding up signs and hoping that Hannah Graham would be found, I recorded the sounds of magic markers squeaking as people were drawing on cardboard. When you hear that squeak, that saves you a lot of time saying, "People are using magic markers and drawing signs."[17]

For his first ever podcast, Augenstein wanted to incorporate different audio elements to craft his story rather than just record the narrative or interviews in a studio.

> That's sort of like a talk show, which I guess would be interesting. But I wanted to make it something that people could visualize and also make it a little bit more of a newsy feel. When I listened to *Serial*, which is very conversational, I thought to myself, I wanted to have some elements of that. I wanted the podcast to be more conversational than just a regular report. I wanted to be able to have some personal insight and share some of those moments, but I didn't want it to be so conversational that it would lose the news credibility. I was aiming for somewhere in between.[18]

Augenstein's experience putting together his first podcast illustrates an important point. Podcasting is not just one thing. It can be whatever you imagine.

Part of *Serial's* great success was that it expanded people's idea of what a podcast could be. True crime and serialized storytelling have been around for ages—think Truman Capote's "In Cold Blood" or "House of Cards" on Netflix. But *Serial* popularized these forms in a new media.

"Telling a serialized story with cliffhangers and plot developments and stuff is not conducive to broadcast radio, because it's difficult for listeners and it's difficult for stations to program," *Serial* co-producer Julie Snyder told *Mother Jones* magazine. "That's the awesome thing with a podcast: We can do a story that unfolds over time. You can either go along—we'll release them every Thursday—or people can binge once they've all been released."[19]

Steve Nelson, former director of on-demand programming for American Public Media and now director of programming at NPR, believes that the explosion of audio production will lead to different types of audio being produced, types that have never been imagined before.

> Things that are interesting to talk about for a small group of people now can find a home and a place that they can gather and talk about whatever it is in a way that you couldn't before or make long-form audio that would never be put on any kind of radio station—commercial, public or otherwise. I think that's great. Secondly, there

[is], you know, the comedy podcast world, the sports podcast world, the public radio podcast world, they're all sort of these little families of other shows. I think the important thing to remember is when people talk about podcasting, a lot of times they think about it in terms of what they listen to. If you're a big sports talk radio fan, you're like, "Oh yeah, I like podcasts." Well, you think podcasts are probably sports talk, and that's great. Public radio folks might think that podcasts all sound like *Serial* and *Invisibilia*, but podcasting is just the vehicle. You can paint that car any way you want and put anything you want into it.[20]

Audio storytelling is only as limited as your imagination and your willingness to push the boundaries.

Find your passion. Find your voice. Find your audience. Podcast.

ACTIVITIES

1. Take your recording equipment outside to record natural sound. Gather a series of identifiable sounds—such as a bell ringing, wind moving through the trees and a child playing on a swing—that will tell a one-to-two-minute story. Don't just record four 30-second segments and stick them together. Linger with the sounds a bit, so that you'll have more pieces to choose from. Figure out where the best place is to hold the microphone, listening on your headphones the entire time. Take as many different pieces as you can to help you tell your story. Save the audio for Activity 6–1.

2. Using only natural sound, tell a story of a process: something with a beginning, a middle and an end. For example, record someone making breakfast. Gather the sounds of coffee being poured into a cup, a spoon stirring sugar into the coffee, toast being dropped into a toaster and then popping up a few minutes later, eggs on a griddle and butter being spread across the toast. Remember to wear your headphones! Save the audio for Activity 6–2.

3. With just one microphone, record a short interview with someone about a significant story from his or her childhood. Focus only on that story. Find out why it was significant for the interviewee, how it made him or her feel at the time and how his or her attitude has changed. Ask, "If you had the chance, would you live the experience over again in the same way, or how would you act differently now?" This is an exercise in listening. Keep your

questions brief, and try not to comment on the interviewee's answers. Focus on letting the interviewee tell the story and building the narrative.

NOTES

1 Campbell, Tiffany (2016, May 21). Phone interview.
2 Ibid
3 Ibid.
4 Ibid.
5 Augenstein, Neal (2016, May 16). Personal interview.
6 Ibid.
7 Ibid.
8 Ibid.
9 Ibid.
10 Ibid.
11 Ibid.
12 Ibid.
13 Ibid.
14 Ibid.
15 Ibid.
16 Ibid.
17 Ibid.
18 Ibid.
19 Lurie, Julia (2014, Sept. 19). "'This American Life' channels 'True Detective' in a new podcast," *Mother Jones*. [www.motherjones.com/media/2014/09/ira-glass-sarah-koenig-julie-snyder-serial-podcast-this-american-life]
20 Nelson, Steve (2016, June 2). Phone interview.

6

Editing

Pulling All the Pieces Together

Although the planning and recording of your first episode will occupy much of your attention during the launch, it's the editing process that will determine how your podcast emerges. Over time, the podcast will evolve, as you bring in new elements and discard old ones. The decisions you make in your early editing sessions will lay the groundwork for what's to come.

There are two interlinking goals when editing audio. The first is to improve the overall quality of the listening experience. This may include removing extraneous background noise to make it easier on the ear or tweaking the audio levels so that all the speakers are talking with the same loudness and clarity.

"As a listener of podcasts, I quickly get turned off if the episode sounds like somebody's in a bathroom stall talking alone," said Ernesto Gluecksmann, co-host of *Through the Noise*.

> You can't get the reflections out if you don't pay attention to making it sound good. I think it becomes a distraction from the content. It might be the best conversation. It might be the best talk or educational content, but if it's distracting with the sound, then I think that's a bad move.[1]

The second goal of audio editing addresses the content side of the podcast. What is it you want to say, and how do you want to say it? Will the story you're telling emerge out of the natural flow of a conversation, or will you compose a narrative out of multiple segments, each tightly edited and self-contained?

This is where some of the decisions you've made about what type of podcast you're doing come into play. If your aim is to create a "natural conversation," perhaps you'll use a light touch in editing, only taking out some of the flubs that happened during recording—or maybe you won't even do that.

"The way we're going for it is a dinner party conversation," Gluecksmann said.

> The "ums," the awkward pauses, all of that adds to the show. It adds to the tension and the entertainment value. We have had to edit some things out. If you go that route, the production costs go up much higher because you have to spend more time getting the edit right and, if you have a really highly produced show, you can go down a rabbit

FIGURE 6.1 Ernesto Gluecksmann and Blake Althen are the hosts of *Through the Noise.*

hole pretty quickly, kind of Frankenstein an episode out because you are trying to cut out all these certain parts.[2]

Glucksmann's aim is to keep *Through the Noise* from sounding too polished, which is what he's told his co-host Blake Althen, who does all the editing.

"I want more of a real conversation," Glucksmann said. "That might be different, I think, with some of the other podcasts that are out there."[3]

When Jay Jacksonrao started *The Nerdpocalypse* podcast, his plan was to create a tightly edited, highly produced show. He quickly discovered the downside of that approach.

What I realized is it took me four hours to edit an hour-and-a-half show. Then [I] said yeah, I'm going to try and just see what happens if we just do it kind of raw. We actually got a better response. Now granted, if we have technical hiccups or something like that, those things get edited out because it is still a professional show. I know some shows don't do that, which I think is a little odd. But for us, as long as the content is there and there's no major hiccups, it runs as is.[4]

Julia Furlan, podcast producer at BuzzFeed, is a big proponent of good editing. She'll typically record between 70 and 90 minutes of audio, sometimes more, for a 30-to-35-minute podcast.

I love a good, edited podcast. It's not easy. It's actually something that is really hard for me. Editing is not an easy skill for me. I love it, but it's not simple. . . . I appreciate the craft of a beautiful edit and I think that it's sometimes lost on people who think they can just talk to their friend on the phone and that's going to be interesting. It's hard to make something interesting. You have to take that stuff out. It goes with the narrative structure.[5]

It's All Journalism began as a "turn the microphones on, record the conversation, add an introduction and do a minimal amount of editing"-type podcast. As we produced more episodes, though, our conversations grew tighter and we made fewer mistakes that had to be removed later.

Over time, we realized there were benefits to doing a shorter, highly edited podcast. If a part of a conversation goes nowhere or is boring, why not take it out? If a guest takes 10 to 15 minutes to feel comfortable and open up, why not start the podcast there, when he suddenly gets more interesting? Or, how about taking the most shocking segment from 30 minutes into the conversation and put it at the beginning in order to hook more listeners?

Some would argue that those types of decisions create content that is not "authentic" or a "real conversation." Some people are looking for long, rambling podcasts, while others just want something entertaining to listen to. Your guest may say something incredible in minute 45, but if you haven't engaged listeners early on, they may not stick around to hear it.

"With every podcast that we produce, we're asking people for a certain percentage of their life," said Laura Mayer, managing producer at Panoply.

> That sounds crazy, but I think that it's true. We're asking for 45 minutes of their day, of their attention, of them really not being able to do much else aside from play Candy Crush or whatever your phone vice of choice is. That is valuable time. Increasingly, with the amount of podcasts out there, we hope that we are giving people options that they feel good about listening to. We don't want to waste their time.[6]

Much of Mayer's early production experience came in public media. She recalled during her early days at Panoply having a conversation with Chief Content Officer Andy Bowers about the podcasting network's approach to editing.

> I remember speaking to Andy and he was saying, "There's a difference between editing podcasts and editing for public radio." With public radio, you have the clock that you have to stick to, or at least you have to know that the clock [is not] as formidable in certain shows anymore. But you have only a certain amount of time. With us, we have as much time as you want. But the flip side of that is you have to learn how to be a different kind of editor.

Having left WNYC and "On the Media" behind, Mayer faced a new challenge—editing without the dictates of a clock.

> At WNYC in general, I learned everything I possibly could have. It was fabulous. But I came here, started editing podcasts and realized that 'six and a half minutes' was tattooed behind my eyelids. I was just so used to like cutting the hell out of things in order to fit a certain time.

And now that there is no specific time you have to hit, there's almost more responsibility on the editor to make smart decisions, because there's no other constraint really, just that the conversation be worthwhile enough to actually have that part remain in the podcast.[7]

At Panoply, the amount of time spent on editing episodes varies depending on the show. An episode of *Slate's Culture Gabfest*, for example, sometimes requires three hours of recording, but the final edited episode comes in at 45 or 50 minutes.

> That's the same with the *Political Gabfest*. They'll record for an hour and a half, two hours, and that will be cut down to around 45 minutes. In terms of time cut out, that's a lot. And I know, with those particular shows, questions will be moved around. We try and make it seem like it's a seamless conversation that has unfolded, but the producer/editor has been spending a lot of time kind of figuring out the ways to make it seem like it's a conversation that just unfolded naturally, but that requires a lot of cutting out of things that didn't help the overall flow of the show for us.[8]

By comparison, *Happier with Gretchen Rubin* doesn't require the same level of editing. Mayer said:

> Gretchen is just kind of the natural host, and she's working with her sister and they talk off mic where they prepare things ahead of time. That is more of a clean-up situation like 'ums,' 'uh,' redos, retakes, that sort of thing. With something like Sophia Amoruso's podcast (*Girlboss Radio*), she has something where, at the top of the show, she has a specific segment with one of her friends that sometimes will end up being seven minutes, and they will sometimes record that for an hour and a half. That's a lot of editing. The same thing goes with the interviews themselves, where Sophia will speak with people for a long time because she wants to be able to have a long conversation with people . . . her editor will cut it down by half.[9]

What the Panoply editors typically cut out, according to Mayer, are irrelevant tangents that lead nowhere or didn't quite get to a point. They'll also remove anything that disrupts the natural flow of a conversation.

> A lot of the time, I'm trying to think back to my days when I was editing the podcast. And that was early days too, when the hosts that

we had weren't really that used to it. We'd edit the whole thing down, listen to it and just realize an entire segment just had to go because it didn't work. That would happen fairly often. It happens less often now because producers are able to spend more time with the host ahead of time to do the prep work.[10]

Malcolm Gladwell's podcast, *Revisionist History*, is a bit of a departure in terms of production for Panoply, Mayer said. The team works off a script written by Gladwell. The editing process begins with a table read, in which he reads the script and the various tracks are played at their appointed moments in the story.

That would be the first editing process, where you'd hear it in a room and then we realized what didn't work, what did work, what there needs [to be] more of, what needs to be restructured. There would be a second draft of the actual episode with his voice in it. Then there would be another round of edits, refining the story, realizing what doesn't work, realizing what there needs to be more [of]. With that particular series, he went through at least six rounds of those sort of edits for each episode.[11]

Jessica Alpert, managing producer for program development at WBUR, takes a similarly intense approach to editing the *Modern Love* podcast. Her goal is to create "a movie for your ears."

The idea was to take the "Modern Love" column, which is in the Sunday Style section of The New York Times and just make it come alive, but through two parts. The first is an actual reading by an actor that's soundscaped and sound designed. The second half is actually a "where are they now" kind of conversation with the "Modern Love" writer, the original essayist. So each episode is about 20 to 25 minutes, and the sound design is extremely intense. There is serious production time put into this project.[12]

Each episode of *Modern Love* mixes music, sound effects, interviews and narration to tell one story in a short amount of time. This requires an eye—and ear—for the details.

Every minute is scrutinized. I mean every sound. Some of them have more music than others. Some are more full of sound effects than others. I like to call it exquisite. It's like a five-star meal. It's the most attention I've ever put on audio in any project. . . . What we bring to the table, what makes it different, is this incredible execution, the skill set of making something beautiful, and so rarely do we have that opportunity these days to actually spend a ton of time making each second beautiful and make it count. Not only was it, we thought, necessary for this project, but it was something that we were excited to do because it's a joy.[13]

The attention to detail Alpert places on the editing of *Modern Love* is likely a rare thing in the podcasting universe and not necessarily something that everyone just starting out in podcasting can achieve. But it's certainly something to which podcasters can aspire.

I know that people slap podcasts together. They sit in their basement and record and that's fine. But I think what we're trying to do here is—just because it's not broadcast doesn't mean it shouldn't have all the loving care that a broadcast has. Actually, this is almost more love and care, because we're not on a clock. We do have deadlines, but we don't have to hit any breaks, and it's really a luxury. This is the only podcast we have that will be this intense in terms of production. We try to get the best sound. We try to avoid phone tape. We try to get people into studios. That's important to us. And I think that's what differentiates us from other producers who maybe don't have our background or don't have access to certain resources. Everything you hear from us will sound really, really good.[14]

REVIEW ALL YOUR RECORDED ELEMENTS

The first thing to do when you start the actual editing process is to determine whether you have all the pieces you need to tell your story. These may include an interview, music, an introduction, an ending tag and natural sound. Depending on how many elements you have, the editing process can become quite involved.

PJ Tobia, a foreign affairs and defense producer at "PBS NewsHour," puts a lot of effort into his podcast, *Shortwave*. For every 8-to-15-minute episode, he has to write a script to wrap around the multiple audio elements and interviews that make up a show.

The interviews, I try to keep each one under 15 minutes. That's going to take me half a day to write the damn thing . . . then my editor gets it. I edit it together, and my editor gets it and I have to make changes. It's usually a good two or three days. When I first started, it would take me forever to do an episode. I've gotten to a place where I'm pretty quick.[15]

Whenever possible, Tobia enlists the help of interns to transcribe the interviews.

What I'll do is while I'm doing the interview—and this is a good TV trick—when you're doing an interview and if you get it, write the time code at which the person said that thing that you think is going to be a sound bite. You get pretty good at figuring out what you want, especially when you keep the interviews short. I just try and do that. I'll write the time code down and then I won't transcribe the whole thing. I'll just search for the bites that I want.[16]

It's All Journalism's structure has evolved over four years. Since it's interview-based, the guest interview forms the core audio for our podcast, but other elements are added to make a complete episode.

First, each episode starts with an audio tease, an interesting quote pulled from our guest interview. It's usually about 30 to 45 seconds long and is designed to hook the listener into playing the entire episode. This is followed by our theme music, which was purchased from a Creative Commons website. [See Appendix A about music rights.] The music then fades into an intro.

The introduction is usually recorded at the beginning of the guest interview and follows a standard format: "Welcome to *It's All Journalism*. I'm Michael O'Connell, here with another podcast about digital media and the people who make it. In studio with me today—." The idea of the intro is to identify the name of the podcast, who you are and what the podcast is about. Then you need to identify the guest and go into why you'll be talking to him or her. This all sets the stage for the conversation you'll be having and tells your audience why they should keep listening.

The intro can also be a place to deal with some of the podcast's "housekeeping," such as advertising special events or letting listeners know how they can sponsor the show or follow it on social media. This is useful information, but avoid overwhelming your audience with extraneous content.

Many podcasts meander through the introduction, chattering about the hosts' lives, before getting to the meat of the discussion. *It's All Journalism's* philosophy is that people are more interested in the topic and the guests than where the host spent his or her vacation or what he OR she had for dinner. Occasionally, we may talk about a conference we're going to or the response to a particular episode, but generally we keep the intro brief and to the point. Remember what Panoply's Laura Mayer said—don't waste your listeners' time.

After the intro comes the main interview. We'll edit out sections that meander and don't make a point, and we'll remove any glitches in the sound. Sometimes we'll move the order of the sections around if it will improve the flow of the conversation.

At the end of the interview, we'll add the outro, which is made up of three parts: A tease to the next episode, our show credits and the theme music. One of the advantages of recording multiple interviews in advance is we know who will be on the following week's show. The outro tease is just a short clip of audio to preview that interview. We'll tag that with a sentence or two about the upcoming guest and then go into our credits. This is where we talk about who worked on the show and where listeners can find our content. Then the theme music brings it all to a close.

HOW TO EDIT AUDIO

Depending on how you recorded your first piece of audio, you may have chosen already which editing software you'll be using.

If you recorded on a laptop, for example, you may have downloaded the free Audacity program or used GarageBand, which is free as well and is already installed on many Apple products. Other editing programs to choose from include Adobe Audition, Cubase Studio, Hindenburg and Pro Tools. All of these offer different features and come in a range of prices, but at the basic level they all follow the same principles when it comes to assembling your podcast. [See Appendix B for a list of editing software.]

Since Audacity is a free, open source editing program that's widely available, it's a good, baseline piece of software for the new podcaster to learn how to edit. For that reason, I'm going to describe how to edit an episode of *It's All Journalism* using Audacity.

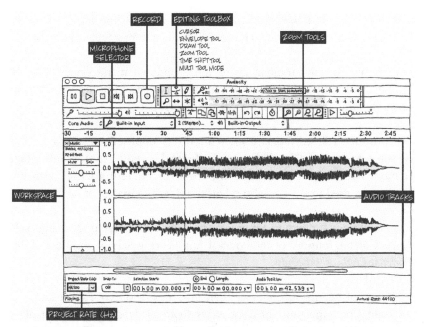

FIGURE 6.2 The Audacity desktop has many of the same features as other audio editing software. The toolbar is at the top, and the central workspace is where you import and edit the audio tracks. Source: This drawing is adapted from the Audacity desktop image Copyright © 2016 Audacity Team.

Open Audacity on your laptop or desktop computer. This will display your workspace. The top section contains your tools; the middle section is where you'll import your audio tracks; and the bottom has a couple of counters to show the position of your cursor within the audio tracks.

If you've ever used a recording device, the controls in the upper left should look familiar. From left to right, they are "Pause," "Play," "Stop," "Rewind," "Fast Forward" and "Record." Remember, you can also use Audacity to record audio by plugging a microphone, mixer or audio interface into your computer's USB port. In the middle of the Audacity workspace is a microphone icon next to a window with a dropdown menu. That's where you can choose the external microphone over the internal microphone.

In the bottom left is a box where you'll select your project's sample rate. A sample rate is how many samples are made per second of the audio. The more samples per second, the better the audio will sound. Choosing 44100 hertz, which is CD quality, should be more than sufficient for a typical podcast.[17]

Under the Audacity toolbar, go to the dropdown menu under "File" to "Import," and import the audio file for your podcast. The file should show up as an audio wave at the center of your workspace.

We produce *It's All Journalism* in mono as opposed to stereo, mostly because it means we'll only have a single track to edit. Another advantage to mono over stereo is that mono files are smaller in terms of the number of bytes compared to stereo—about half the size, as a matter of fact.[18]

"You could mix it down to a mono, or you could do stereo podcasting," said Chris Curran, founder of the Podcast Engineering School and host of *The Podcast Engineering Show.*

> Plenty of people still put out their episodes in stereo. I do. I know Todd Cochrane [host of *Geek News Central*] does. I know a lot of people do, especially if you have music. The music is usually in stereo, and it sounds good in stereo. When you collapse it down to mono, it sounds very dull and with no depth or dimension. It just sounds one-dimensional.[19]

Unless you have a need for stereo, such as including a lot of music, then producing in mono should do the job.

FIGURE 6.3 Longtime audio engineer Chris Curran is the host of *The Podcast Engineering Show.*

If you want to produce a stereo podcast, you can import and edit stereo tracks. But you need to make sure that as you're working, you select and edit both tracks at the same time so that they remain in sync. You can also do all your editing in stereo and mix it down into mono at the end if you want.

But, for the sake of the demonstration, let's create a mono podcast.

Most of the time we'll record it in mono, but if we do record it in stereo we'll mix the stereo file down at the beginning of the editing process. To do that in Audacity, go to "Tracks" in the toolbar and click on "Stereo Track to Mono" in the dropdown menu.

Be sure to inspect the audio wave to make sure there are no obvious differences in the voices you've recorded on the track. The wave should fill up the middle portion of the display, generally between 0.5 and –0.5. If the audio was recorded too low and shows up too close to the centerline (0.0), you can amplify the entire wave. Go to "Edit" and "Select All," then under "Effect" choose "Amplify," moving the amplification slider to the right to reach the desired level. You can also use the "Cursor Tool," which looks like the capital letter "I" in your toolbox, to select specific portions of the audio wave to amplify.

If the entire audio wave fills up too much of the display, extending nearly to or touching 1.0 or –1.0, you can select the entire wave and use "Amplify" to lower it. You'll move the amplification slider to the left, decreasing the level of the wave.

Another way to adjust to the entire wave is with the "Envelope Tool," which is located between the "Cursor" and the "Pencil Tool"—it looks something like an hourglass. Click on the "Envelope Tool" and then click once on the top or bottom of the audio wave. The entire wave should contract in unison, allowing you to set it to the level you desire.

All of these neat little adjustments can address some of your audio quality problems. However, they also can create new ones. If you've recorded the track at too low a level, when you amplify it, the audio may sound muddy. Likewise, if you've recorded it too high, when you decrease the level, the audio might sound clipped in places. The only way to ensure that your audio is going to sound its best is to make sure you record it properly in the first place. There's only so much you can do during the editing process to clean up the sound. Curran said:

> The golden rule of audio engineering is record it properly the first time. Period. Because if you don't record it properly, then you're going to have to get into all these fixes and tricks and techniques and plugins. You're going to have to jump through nine hoops to make it sound better, but it still won't sound great. So the idea is record it right the first time.[20]

Once you've made fixes to the entire wave, begin listening back to the audio to see whether there are any portions you need to edit out because of flubs or unnecessary content. You'll be using the "Cursor" to select the portions of the audio you want to take out. Drop the "Cursor" at the beginning of the section you wish to take out, right click and drag to the end of the area you wish to remove to highlight it. Then key in "Command+X" or select "Cut" in the dropdown menu under "Edit" in your toolbar. To make it easier for you to view where to position the "Cursor" when you're editing, use the "Zoom" tools, which look like magnifying glasses, to zoom in and out of the audio wave. Continue to the end of the audio wave, making edits as you go along.

As you're editing, resist the temptation to remove all the breaths from the audio. It will sound weird if the person continues to talk but never stops to breathe, especially if he's talking for a very long time. Also, removing the breaths without replacing an equal amount of blank sound will increase the pace of speech, which also sounds weird.

Sometimes, though, the person speaking will be a heavy breather, and you may need to do something about it to keep it from becoming too much of a distraction to your audience. One trick I've picked up is to remove a small portion from the middle of the breath. Use the "Zoom In" tool to magnify the breath, then cut out the middle third of it using your "Cursor." If you listen back, the remaining breath will be hardly noticeable.

To move sections of audio within the same track, use the "Cursor" to select and "Copy" ("Command+C") the section you want to move, "Cut" ("Command+X") it from its original location and drop the "Cursor" into the new spot. Then, key in "Command+V" or select "Paste" in the dropdown menu under "Edit" to place the track in its new location.

Once you've finished editing your main audio track, it's time to add the other audio elements to your podcast. For the demonstration, let's add the theme music and the introduction to the beginning of the podcast.

Under "File," import the theme music as a new audio track, which will show up as a wave form under the audio you just finished editing. Both the music and your main audio track will be flush with the left side of the workspace. If you played it now, the music would drown out the speech on your main audio track. You'll need to reposition your main audio so that listeners will hear only the music.

In your toolbox, click on the "Time Shift Tool," which looks like a horizontal line with two arrows on either end. Then, click on your main audio track. You should be able to slide the entire wave to the right and out of the way for the moment.

Next, import your introduction as a new audio track. This will show up below your music track. Using the "Time Shift Tool," slide the introduction so that it overhangs about five seconds of the end of the music track.

What we want to do is fade the music out so that it plays under the introduction without drowning it out. To do this, position the "Envelope Tool" on the music track where you want the music to begin to fade. Click once. This will place a dot on the top and bottom of the music track. Next, move the "Envelope Tool" to the end of the music track and click again, placing another dot there. If you slide the "Envelope Tool" along the track, it will begin to close. Play with it a little bit to get it to fade at the rate you want.

Next, use the "Time Shift Tool" to slide your main audio to where it touches the end of the introduction. No need to do anything fancy here. The introduction is going to flow straight into the main audio.

If you haven't found it yet, there's a slider at the bottom of the workspace that allows you to travel to the end of all your audio tracks. Slide that to the right to get to the end of your main audio. Following the same procedure you used to add the theme music and introduction to the beginning of the podcast, add your outro and any other elements you want to include at the end.

Now that you understand how to move elements around using multiple tracks, you can use this procedure to add elements to the middle of your

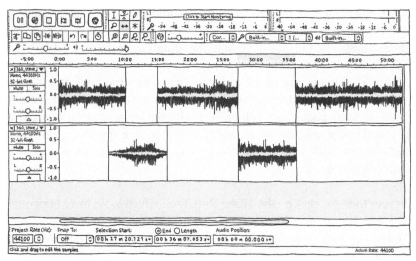

FIGURE 6.4 This drawing of the Audacity desktop shows two tracks of audio being edited together. Both tracks have been cut into segments, and the "Envelope Tool" is being used to fade in and out the leftmost audio in the bottom track. Source: This drawing is adapted from the Audacity desktop Copyright © 2016 Audacity Team.

main audio. In this scenario, within your main audio track, find the place you want to insert the new audio and drop the "Cursor." Then, in the dropdown menu under "Edit" go to "Clip Boundaries" and select "Split." Your main audio track is now cut into two pieces.

Use the "Time Shift Tool" to slide the right piece out of the way. Then, import your new audio track and reposition it with the "Time Shift Tool" so that it lines up with the open space you've created in your main audio. If you want to, you can use the "Envelope Tool" to fade in or fade out the audio. Once you've finished all your additions, go to "Clip Boundaries" in the dropdown menu of "Edit" and select "Join." This will link up all your content.

Once you've made all your additions and edits, it's time to prepare the podcast for export. The first thing you'll need to do is equalize the low and high frequencies of your audio. In Audacity, go to "Equalization" in the dropdown menu under "Effect." Curran said:

> One thing that most podcasters don't do is take out some of the really low end. So a lot of the bass frequencies, the really low bass frequencies, probably 80 or 100 hertz or lower, you need to roll

them off—meaning decrease them a little bit, because a lot of micro-phones out of the box will sound a little bassy. They'll have a lot of bass in it. If you remove some of that low bass, then it makes the voice clearer.[21]

Go ahead and try the automatic setting in Audacity's equalization tool. Listen to your track in a few different places to see how it sounds. If you don't like it, you can "Undo" it under "Edit" and then try to adjust the "Equalization" settings so that it sounds how you like it.

Next, go to "Compressor" in the dropdown menu under "Effect" and click "OK." This will compress the dynamic range of the audio so that distance between the loudest and softest parts of the track is reduced. That way, your audience is not turning the volume up and down as the vocals change. Curran said:

> When you compress it a little bit, it compresses it into, let's say, a 10 dB zone, where you can hear each voice and you can hear it well. That's the function of a compressor. It just tightens everything up and controls it a little better, so it's not really loud and then really soft.[22]

Now you're ready to export. First, save your project to your computer. Then, under "File," select "Export Audio" or key in "Shift+Command+E." In the new window, give the file a name and then choose "MP3" as the format. Next, open the "Options" button to specify your MP3 options. Select "Constant" for your "Bit Rate Mode."

Under "Quality" you'll need to make a choice of what your fixed bit rate will be. Although a higher number means the quality of your audio will be better, the size of the file will be much bigger too. The size of your file impacts how much space you'll be taking up on your audio server and determines how long it will take listeners to download an episode. From a quality standpoint, you don't want the number to be too low; from a storage and user experience standpoint, you don't want it to be too high.

For mono recording, 64 kilobits per second (Kbps) will give you AM radio quality sound, which is good for podcasts with a lot of vocals, and 96 Kbps will produce FM quality, which is good for podcasts that combine vocals with other elements, such as bumpers and music. For stereo recording, 128 Kbps will give you CD quality, and 192 Kbps or higher will deliver high-end audio.[23]

Once you've figured out the best "Quality" level for your needs, select "Joint Stereo" as your "Channel Mode" and save.

Audacity then gives you the option to add "Metadata" to your track, such as "Artist Name," "Track Title" and "Album Title." You don't need to fill out all the fields, but you should include some information to help identify the MP3 file when it's downloaded. Otherwise, if no metadata is present, some audio players will display "Unknown Artist" or "Unknown Title," which isn't very useful to your listeners and doesn't help you grow your brand.[24]

Once you've added your "Metadata" and clicked "OK," Audacity will mix down your edited audio into an MP3 file and then you're done.

Your first podcast episode will not be perfect. In fact, you'll probably need to listen to multiple episodes to perceive the difference in sound and figure out how to improve the recording and editing. Curran said:

> You record a podcast. Listen to it. Put it onto your phone. Put the MP3 on your phone [and] listen to [it with] your earbuds. Go into your car. Listen to it in your car. Listen on a boom box. Listen on a little Bluetooth speaker—whatever. Listen in a bunch of different places and you'll hear different things. You'll say, "Wow." Especially when you go in the car, if you listen in the car. That's when you'll notice the bass. You'll be like, "Oh my God, there's all this low end." It's so muddy, and it sounds so huge and almost unintelligible, because in your car you have big speakers with better bass. If you listen on little earbuds, the bass might not bother you, because you might not even hear it.[25]

Curran recommends making incremental tweaks over time to improve the quality of your sound.

"If you take every episode for the first 10 episodes, listen in different places and then make tiny adjustments for the next episode, you'll dial it in over 10 episodes," he said. "You'll tweak it and then it'll be really good."[26]

Editing may not be the sexiest part of podcasting, but it may be the most important. It's the place where all of your planning, research, interviewing, recording and writing come together to create a podcast episode to entertain and enlighten your audience. It's often a challenge, but it can also be immensely rewarding as you become more proficient. If you put the time and care into becoming a good editor, the effort will show. Alpert said:

> I have a lot to say about these podcasts that are people who sit in their basement, because some of them are great and some of them could be great if they were just more disciplined about the editing process. I think things could be much more tightly edited, even if it's just two people just yapping away. I feel like there's something to be said about really thinking about your listener and [asking] are you repeating yourself? Is this redundant? I just think there's a lot of laziness out there around that, and it's not that hard to do. Well, maybe it is hard to be a good editor, but I just think that even if you're just slapping it together, it deserves a nice, nice edit.[27]

ACTIVITIES

1. Record a new audio track in which you tell a brief story. It can be anything you want—a joke or something sad, for example—but keep it to under two minutes in length. Then, take the audio you recorded for Activity 5–1 and use it as background sound for your story. You'll need to import multiple audio tracks, cut segments and fade in the natural sound to change scenes. Be creative.

2. Edit together the audio you collected for Activity 5–2 into a one-minute story. Then, record a short piece of music that you think reflects the story of the audio you collected. Now, using your editing program, import the music tracks and blend them together, fading the sound in and out and cutting segments.

NOTES

1 Gluecksmann, Ernesto (2016, May 6). Personal interview.
2 Ibid.
3 Ibid.
4 Jacksonrao, Jay (2016, June 13). Skype interview.
5 Furlan, Julia (2016, June 10). Phone interview.
6 Mayer, Laura (2016, June 8). Phone interview.
7 Ibid.
8 Ibid.
9 Ibid.
10 Ibid.
11 Ibid.

12 Alpert, Jessica (2016, June 17). Phone interview.

13 Ibid.

14 Ibid.

15 Tobia, PJ (2016, June 16). Phone interview.

16 Ibid.

17 "MP3 (MPEG Layer 3) tips for podcasting" (2016). *Blubrry*. [https://create.blu-brry.com/manual/creating-podcast-media/audio/mp3-mpeg-layer-3-tips/]

18 Ibid.

19 Curran, Chris (2016, Aug. 17). Phone interview.

20 Ibid.

21 Ibid.

22 Ibid.

23 "MP3."

24 "Editing podcasts" Educational technology for healthcare education, (2012). The University of Nottingham, United Kingdom. [http://nottingham.ac.uk/nmp/sonet/resources/podcasting/podcast_editing.html#metadata]

25 Curran.

26 Ibid.

27 Alpert.

7

Where Will Your Podcast Live Online?

Now that you've finished editing your first podcast episode, it's time to post it online. But where should your podcast live?

In truth, your podcast is going to have two homes. The first is your website, where you'll post information about your podcast. This could include photos, write-ups, show notes, advertising, a calendar for events, anything you want with the exception of your audio. That's going to live on a media server, typically a podcasting platform designed to host audio and video files.

You may be tempted to load your audio onto your website, but don't do it. Your website server will not be up to the task of hosting your MP3s and other large media files and making them available quickly when your audience wants to download the latest episode. Although podcasts can be downloaded around the clock, most of your traffic will occur within the first three days of an episode's release. A website server would be quickly overrun with the spike in demand, and service to those just visiting your website would be negatively impacted as well. Remember: Never post your podcast to your main website.[1]

Instead, choose from a number of podcast hosting platforms, such as Libsyn, Blubrry, Podbean and audioBoom. Some, such as SoundCloud, allow you to post a limited amount of audio files per month for free. But, if you anticipate posting a lot of audio in a month and want to access more services, such as advanced data analytics, it's worthwhile to pay for a hosting platform that will provide all of that.

HOW TO CHOOSE A WEBSITE FOR YOUR PODCAST

Cesar Abeid is a happiness engineer at Automattic, the company behind WordPress. Besides having the best job title ever, he hosts the *Project Management for the Masses* podcast.

> Project management is basically the secret formula that big companies like Apple and Google use to take an idea and turn that into a product. So every year, the CEO for Apple, Mr. Tim Cook, will get up on the stage and take a device out of his pocket and say, "This is the next iPhone or iGadget." And then he's going to say, "You'll be able to buy this and on this date, and you'll be able to pay this much for it." And year after year, he delivers on that promise. Right?[2]

Abeid's podcast gleans lessons from master project managers at companies like Apple and Google to help his audience deliver on whatever they promised to their families, their colleagues or whomever.

> More and more people are finding themselves in this situation. They're asked by their boss or by their employer: "Hey, we need to have a social media plan for the launch of our next product. I want a budget. I want a deadline from you by next week." Right. So work is getting more complicated in a way that we have to make these estimates and we have to create these things out of thin air. . . . And I think we are ill equipped as human beings to make those things from the top of our head.[3]

According to Abeid, project management provides a set of tools and methods that help people break huge tasks down into workable chunks in order to meet their deadlines. Project management, in fact, is a great skill for podcasters who are trying to deliver on the promise they made to their audience of producing great content on time.

Beginning podcasters know they need to get their podcast online and maybe create a website. But they also have to find a place for their audio to live and get an RSS feed for iTunes and other podcatchers, which are computer programs that automatically download podcasts for their users. What if they want to monetize the podcast and promote it? Taken together, all these tasks seem like a big mountain to climb. But it's really not a mountain. It's just lots of little steps.

Abeid agreed. "And not only that, I think there is work that is project and there is work that we call operations," he said.

> For example, the launch of the podcast is a project. It has a beginning. It has an end to create something unique. The ongoing promotion and creation of the content—that is more like operations, because you don't have an end in sight. I particularly don't like that kind of work. I like having a deadline and having something to check off.[4]

When Abeid launched *Project Management for the Masses*, he treated the entire podcast as one big project, rather than just focusing on the launch as the end goal.

> I made a promise on my first episode that I was going to do 20 episodes, and at the end that would be it. Unless things changed along the way or I liked it so much that I want[ed] to do more. But, I made that promise, so in my mind that's the thing. If you're going to start a podcast, it's overwhelming to think: "I'm going to be doing this forever. And what if I don't like it? What if something happens? What if I can't do it? I'm going to disappoint my audience." But, if you have an end in sight, then it's easier for you to internalize that as something that is manageable. It's a lot easier also to break them down into more manageable chunks and learn what to delegate, what you need to do it yourself, and because you know you have an end in sight.[5]

One of the integral chunks of launching a podcast is having a website to grow your brand and to which you can direct your audience for the latest news about your podcast. It's a necessary thing.

For a lot of people, building a website seems like an unscalable mountain. But remember the strategies of project management: Little steps.

Tiffany Campbell, executive editor for digital at WBUR, the public radio station in Boston, spends much of her day figuring out how to make audio thrive online. She suggests that beginning podcasters start out as "lo-fi" as possible when choosing where to post their audio.

> If you're just starting out, getting it onto one of the platforms that does all the hosting for you is a great place to start. SoundCloud, Libsyn, something like that is a full-meal deal, where you can upload, host. It all lives nicely in this thing. It can be shareable. Those are things that you don't want to mess with until you feel a lot more confident. That helps you with distribution, because you're already in that ecosystem.[6]

Campbell stressed the importance of maintaining an online presence separate from your audio hosting platform. That's where you can build your podcast's identity, conduct all your promotion and talk directly to your audience.

> I'm also a big believer that you shouldn't lock yourself up in these walled gardens either. Creating even just a Tumblr blog or an out-of-the-box simple website, where you can put this audio on so that you can share it more easily. Think about if you're sharing it with your mom or something else. She's not going to go into SoundCloud. It's going to be foreign for her. If you can send her a link where the audio lives, she's going to be able to—not to pick on moms, because moms can be totally tech savvy—you want to make it so dead simple for people to consume.[7]

As Campbell suggests, Tumblr is a good choice for a first-time podcaster, but so is setting up a Facebook page dedicated to your podcast. Both platforms are easy to use and naturally tie into your social media circles. Once you've chosen a hosting service for your podcast, you can share the episode on Facebook or Tumblr or, if your service offers them, place an embeddable player on the page.

The next step up is building a simple blog-type website, using a service like WordPress or Squarespace. Both services offer a variety of templates, some of which are specifically designed for podcasts. They'll also guide you through the process of obtaining a new domain, which is the "name" of your web address, or linking an existing domain to your page.

WordPress was a natural choice for the *It's All Journalism* podcast, because the three producers already had experience with the platform, having been required to build WordPress pages as part of American University's Interactive Journalism program. We purchased our domain name [ItsAllJournalism.com] at GoDaddy, which we decided to use as our hosting server. The hosting server is where your actual website lives. When you download updates and files to your WordPress page, they're stored on your hosting server. Abeid said:

> I think every single podcast that I've ever known, maybe with one exception or two, they have a WordPress site, and outside of podcasting, WordPress powers 26 percent of the entire web. So one in every four websites that exist today is WordPress. It's mind boggling. The result is that it's well adopted and there's a lot of support. There's a lot of documentation.[8]

For the first year and a half, *It's All Journalism* used a blog-style template, which we customized using plugins. A plugin is a widget that adds new elements to your page, like a media player or social media feed. We used an audio player plugin so that people could play our podcast on our page. Abeid said:

> I remember when I was growing up in Brazil, everybody drove a VW bug. Everybody knew how to fix them. And it was a no-nonsense car that got you from here to there. So, in a way, WordPress is like the VW bug. It's highly customizable. Everybody knows how to fix it; if you need help with it, you can . . . pay somebody to fix it. Anybody can do it right now. Any web developer can fix a WordPress site.[9]

Eventually, we decided to update our page and purchased a template from Appendipity, a company that designs WordPress themes catering to a podcasting audience.

"When we design a theme, we always keep that in mind that this is for a podcaster," said Joey Kissimmee, a marketer and podcaster whose company, Income Press, created Appendipity.

> Essentially, it's just a blog theme, a WordPress theme. You can do everything you can with a regular WordPress theme: blogging and videos and all that stuff. It's just catered more towards the podcasters, because we, as podcasters, we want our podcast to shine and be focused, and that's what our theme does. It helps focus your attention on your podcast front and center.[10]

One of the things Todd Cochrane, CEO and founder of RawVoice and its podcasting service Blubrry, has been telling podcasters from the beginning is that they need to build their brand. Where they need to do that is on their own website, so that they have a place to send listeners.

"You have to have your space," he said. "It doesn't matter who you host with. I want you to host with Blubrry, but I want you to have your own dot-com to build your own brand."[11]

One of the nice things that Blubrry offers is a free WordPress page for all of its customers. WordPress is one of the most popular website platforms in the world. It's fairly easy to use and customize. Blubrry also provides the free PowerPress plugin, which links the WordPress audio player to your episodes stored on Blubrry.

> You can use the tools that we provide, like PowerPress, to make it easy to, number one, control your own intellectual property. Number two, we save you time in posting. You basically write a blog post. You upload your media right from within your WordPress dashboard and then you hit publish. And that's really the moniker of what I say: "Post, upload, publish" is our claim to fame. Step one, two, three, done. You have to get that stuff set up initially, which takes a little bit.[12]

Although your podcast episodes are going to be stored on a separate server, your audio can still have a presence on your website, either through links or through embeddable players, which most platforms include as part of their service. Campbell said:

> Once you have that going and you're more comfortable with your production, [you may think] "I want to host myself. I want to do my own RSS feeds. I want to control my distribution a little bit more." But I think when you're just starting out, that's much too much of an ask. You want to think about building audience first. Once you get a bigger audience, then you can start thinking about "How do I really want to control my distribution?"[13]

WHAT TO LOOK FOR IN A PODCAST HOSTING SERVICE

Blubrry is the podcasting hosting service that *It's All Journalism* uses. Way back in 2012, I did a cursory investigation and discovered that it wouldn't be a good idea to post our podcasts directly to our website server, which is what I originally was going to do. In my review of the options available, Blubrry seemed to be the best fit for our needs, and it's worked out well since.

This isn't meant to be an endorsement. Many of the podcasters I interviewed for this book use other platforms, such as Libsyn, Podbean and SoundCloud. All said they were quite happy with the service they received.

Hosting services offer a variety of resources for the beginning podcaster, ranging from online support and tutorials to helping you set up a website to providing an embeddable player or building an app for your subscribers to share or download. As you're comparing the different hosting services, there are a few basic considerations to keep in mind.

"Bandwidth and storage space should be top considerations when evaluating hosting options," Shannon Martin, Podbean's communications director, wrote in a blog post.[14]

Bandwidth refers to how much information can be transferred through a network. "Every time someone downloads an episode of your podcast, it uses bandwidth," Martin wrote. "The bigger your podcast files, the more bandwidth they use. The more people who listen to your podcast, the more bandwidth it uses."[15]

Storage is just what it sounds like. How much storage can you get for the best price? You need to calculate how much storage you'll need each month, so that you'll have no problems uploading on a regular basis. For example, a typical episode of *It's All Journalism* runs about 35 minutes, which equates to about a 36-megabyte MP3. If we post four episodes a month, we'll need approximately 144 megabytes of storage at minimum. Occasionally, we'll post bonus episodes, so we need to tack on another 100 megabytes per month to give us a little wiggle room.

Although bandwidth and storage size are good ways to evaluate which is the best service for you, the most important reason to choose a hosting service is to get a reliable RSS feed.

As mentioned in the introduction, the RSS feed is the line of code you send to media players like iTunes and Google Play and podcatchers such as Stitcher and Overcast. Those are the places listeners go to download or

FIGURE 7.1 Shannon Martin is communications director at Podbean.

subscribe to podcasts. The RSS feed tells the different media players and podcatchers when you've posted a new episode, so that your fans can enjoy it without having to go look for it. For that reason, you want to choose a hosting service that's going to maintain your RSS feed and give you the freedom to take it with you wherever you go online.

"Libsyn's not going to get in the way of your content," said Robert Walch, Libsyn's vice president of podcaster relations and host of *podCast411*.

> [Other services aren't] going to give you full control of the RSS feed. If you ever want to leave Libsyn, you're fully able to leave. No one's ever hosted with Libsyn and lost their audience. There are other services out there that won't let you forward on your feed. . . . The most important thing as a podcaster is your RSS feed. It's not your website. It's not anything else. It's your RSS feed. That's the most important thing. You have to have a good RSS feed.[16]

Libsyn is the largest and oldest of the podcast hosting services.

> Libsyn was the first podcast hosting company. Luckily enough, that's helped us become the biggest. We'll deliver over 25 percent of all the download requests and streams that come through iTunes and podcast apps this year. No one else is over 10 percent, to put it in perspective.[17]

Libsyn hosts some of the biggest names in podcasting, including the NFL, Marc Maron, Joe Rogan and the Nerdist Network.

According to Walch, Libsyn's strength is its reliability. "When the president came on Marc Maron's podcast and he got a million downloads in less than 48 hours, they called us up a week before and said, 'Hey, we're going to have the president on next week; do you guys need to do anything?' We were like, 'Nope. We're fine,'" he said. "It wasn't even a blip on the radar, or barely a blip on the radar. It didn't cause any issues at all. We didn't do anything different. It came out, was delivered and had no issues."[18]

Most platforms offer statistical information to their customers about the number of downloads an episode received. According to Walch, Libsyn goes even deeper, providing its customers with statistics on how many times an episode was requested and where it was requested geographically, down to the city level.

> That's why a lot of comedians like Libsyn. They're able to see, "I've got this many downloads coming from St. Louis versus this many in Indianapolis versus this many in Kansas City." They can see where their audiences are, so that they can use that information and show it to nightclub managers at different comedy clubs to get bookings.[19]

Libsyn also provides statistics on user agents, like how many episodes are being downloaded to Apple's Podcasts player or other players like Overcast and Shifty Jelly's Pocket Casts. As of July 2016, Libsyn statistics can also tell customers how many of their downloads originate from Facebook, Twitter, LinkedIn and Tumblr.

> We can see, based on the destinations, where that consumption is. Not just user agents, destinations. Rather than saying, "Wow, I got all these Safari downloads and all these Mozilla downloads and all these Firefox downloads," now you'll be able to say, "These came from

Facebook. These came from Twitter. These came from LinkedIn."
That will help you better in your marketing efforts.[20]

Libsyn customers can put the HTML5 embeddable player on their websites,
so that their customers can play the audio there or share it out on social
media. Customers can also get smartphone apps customized to their show.

> I feel as a podcaster, you should have a smartphone app for your show,
> and that [app], again, is its own special destination. You can publish
> special content just to your app. Apps, I believe, are really vital, because
> most people still just listen to a few podcasts. Seventy-nine percent
> of podcast listeners listen to five or fewer podcasts. They don't need
> aggregator apps. If they like your show, you get that app on their home-
> screen. That keeps you more in their mind than anything else.[21]

Libsyn offers five pricing plans based on monthly storage use, from 50 megabytes for $5 to 1,500 megabytes for $75. "We don't have any free services,"
Walch said. "That's why we're still in business after 11 years."

The podcasting apps are available only to customers who sign up for one of
Libsyn's Advanced Plans, which start at the 400 megabyte/$20 level. If you
want an app, you'll have to pay an additional $10 a month. Plus, you'll need
to create developer accounts at both iTunes and Google Play.

> They're easy to get, and they have a tutorial that explains how to get
> them. It walks you through all those tough parts. It's just a bunch of
> steps. Not difficult. Upload some artwork and then we build the app
> and put it into your developer account.[22]

Libsyn also offers customers a customizable podcasting page and themes.
Beginning podcasters can use that page as a website where they can send
their listeners to learn more about the show.

Blubrry's Todd Cochrane has a simple reason why beginners should choose
his service over others. "My team is made up of podcasters," he said. "Every
team member that is at Blubrry has done a podcast. You're not on a team
unless you have [done] or will [do a podcast]. We understand what it takes
to build a show."[23]

Like Libsyn, Blubrry doesn't offer free storage. Pricing plans begin at $12
a month for 100 megabytes of storage, all the way up to $80 for 1,000

megabytes. Blubrry also offers unlimited storage for businesses at a premium price.

Unlike Blubrry or Libsyn, Podbean, which has been around for about 10 years, offers a free option for people who just want to stick their toe into the podcasting pond.

"Especially if a student or someone is just getting started out that really has no idea—'Do I want to even do this?'—sign up for a free account," Martin offered. "It's limited in storage space and bandwidth, but it's certainly a great way to give it a try to see if you like the platform. So it's really quick to sign up and easy."[24]

At Podbean, $3 a month will get you 100 megabytes of storage and 100 gigabytes of bandwidth. Price plans go all the way up to $29 a month, which gets you unlimited audio and video storage and unmetered bandwidth. If you're a podcasting network or a large organization, Podbean offers a Network level plan for $199 a month. According to Martin, most people sign up for the $9 a month plan, which gets you unlimited storage (audio only) and unmetered bandwidth.

Like the other hosting services, Podbean provides comprehensive statistics, iTunes support and an RSS feed. Customers also receive their own website, with a variety of podcast themes to choose from. At all paid plan levels, Podbean offers embeddable players and an Android/iPhone app.

> We offer a place for people to upload their audio files, store with us on the cloud, and we make sure that all the back end, all the technical stuff, is taken care of, so that their files are served up easily to the people that want to listen. So they don't have reliability issues, and that's what media hosting is all about. You don't want to run your own server and do that. It's a nightmare. We even have huge companies that come to us and use podcasting for internal communications, and they don't even do it, even though they have a massive server farm. That's the primary thing we offer.[25]

Many of Podbean's customers are beginners who don't have a lot of technical knowledge about posting audio or building a website.

> It's very simple, but we also offer more and more ancillary features, so even if people aren't hosted on our platform, we have an advertising

marketplace and a crowdfunding [option]. So we're doing a lot of things with monetization for any and all podcasters no matter where they're hosted.[26]

Podbean's monetization support comes in the form of a crowdfunding service, similar to Kickstarter, Indiegogo and Patreon, but tied specifically to podcasting.

> That's a way to raise funds from your listeners, so listeners can support your show. The advertising marketplace, which has just launched, brand new, is a place online where podcasters and businesses can meet. So a business, who might already advertise on podcasts or might just think it's a good idea, can come to the marketplace, find someone appropriate, even find a relatively small podcast but [one] that fits their niche maybe, and they say, "I don't have a huge advertising budget." Our goal in launching that was to meet the needs potentially of everyone by just being a space to connect for that.[27]

One of the quick, easy—and free—ways to get a podcast up online and obtain an RSS feed is to post on SoundCloud. *It's All Journalism* started posting its weekly podcast there a year after we launched on Blubrry. At the time, we had signed a content-sharing agreement with the Association of Alternative Newsmedia, and their website didn't have a built-in audio player. We signed up with SoundCloud to take advantage of its embeddable player, which Blubrry didn't offer at the time—it does now. We continued to use Blubrry as our primary hosting service to maintain our RSS feed and receive statistical data. We decided to post on SoundCloud to widen our availability beyond just relying on our website and iTunes to list episodes.

SoundCloud offers 3 hours of audio storage to its customers for a free, 30-day trial. All you have to do is sign up and upload your audio to obtain a simple page that displays audio players for each of your episodes. As with a regular blog-style website, you get a landing page, and each episode has its own page where you can include text and links. It's very basic but functional. You also get embeddable players and Twitter cards, which you can cut and paste and embed in the various social networks. Most importantly, you get an RSS feed you can send to iTunes and other listing services.

If, after 30 days, you decide you want to continue to use SoundCloud, there are three payment levels. At the Basic Level, you get three hours a month of uploading and the minimal level of statistics for free. The Pro Level, which costs $7 a month, gets you six hours of uploading plus more detailed statistics. With the Pro Level, you get unlimited uploads and statistics that show from which websites and apps your subscribers are playing your episodes.[28]

Spreaker is another hosting platform, one that goes a step further—it provides apps that allow you to do live recordings and broadcasts.

"Obviously, that's tied in to that distribution, so you can connect to social networks and have everything automatically publish to those networks," said Anna Piazza, community and marketing manager at Spreaker. "We offer an embeddable player to embed into your website. We give an RSS feed, so that you can plug that into different podcatchers like iTunes and Stitcher."[29]

Everything that's recorded through Spreaker's apps is automatically saved to the customer's account, where it can then be sorted into multiple shows.

> We also offer measurements . . . some statistics on plays, who's listened to you while you were live. Where were they listening to you from? Was it from iTunes, or was it from Spreaker's website? We also offer some geolocation stats, so cities and countries that your listeners are coming from, and male to female and age demographics as well.[30]

Bandwidth, storage, embeddable players, apps, different levels of statistical information, live recording and price—a podcaster has many things to consider when choosing a hosting service. The best advice is to figure out which service best matches your needs and to talk to other podcasters about their experiences with the different platforms. A free option might be a good place to test the water. Or you may want to go all-in. But even if you make the "wrong" decision, many of the platforms make it easy for you to maintain your RSS feed and migrate your content to another server.

YOU HAVE ARRIVED

Getting on iTunes is the big moment of arrival for a many podcasters, so savor it.

You've planned, recorded and edited your podcast and uploaded it to a hosting service. Now you have an RSS feed, which makes it very easy to get listed on iTunes.

Go to the Apple store and follow the instructions.[31] It'll ask you to test your RSS feed. Once that's been cleared—which usually takes a few seconds—you can submit your feed and podcast artwork.

Your podcast artwork should be square, with a minimum size of 1400 by 1400 pixels to a maximum of 3000 by 3000 pixels. It should be in .jpg or .png format, with RGB color.[32]

As far as the subject of your artwork, that's up to you. Remember, though, this will be the first impression many people will have of you. Make it good.

Even though you've arrived, you want your podcast to grow, and that means promotion and maybe figuring out how to make it sustainable. That's the next mountain to climb.

ACTIVITIES

1. Once you've recorded your first podcast, estimate how much storage you'll need to post a month's worth of audio. For example, if your podcast is 30 minutes long and you'll be posting four episodes a month, you'll need 120 minutes of storage—about 56.6 megabytes. Make a list of what other features are important to you, such as embeddable players, apps, a free website, social media sharing and good data analytics. Compare the different hosting services to determine which one best meets your needs and fits in your budget.

2. Investigate which website option is the best for you. Can you get by with a Facebook or Tumblr page, or do you want to launch a blog page using WordPress or Squarespace? Compare some of the websites offered by the various hosting services. If you want your own domain, type a fitting domain name—such as ilike2podcast.com or thebaconpod.com—into a browser to see whether it's already taken. If it's not, you can go to a domain registrar like GoDaddy or Bluehost to purchase the domain. Some registrars also host websites. You can build your website using WordPress or Squarespace and either migrate the files to the new hosting server or just update the domain name.

3. Once you've edited your podcast, ask five people whose opinions you trust to listen to it and give you feedback. You can send them the audio file or, if you've already posted it, send them the link. Praise is nice, but you

want to receive constructive criticism. Ask them what they thought of the audio quality and editing. Find out whether they were engaged throughout the entire episode or whether they lost interest at some point. If they did lose interest, ask when it happened. Discover what they liked about it and what they didn't like about it. Again, you should be happy that you've posted your first podcast, but episode 1 is just the starting point. Each episode should be better than the last.

NOTES

1 "Media podcast hosting," (2017). *Blubrry*. [https://create.blubrry.com/manual/internet-media-hosting/]
2 Abeid, Cesar (2016, July 7). Personal interview.
3 Ibid.
4 Ibid.
5 Ibid.
6 Campbell, Tiffany (2016, May 21). Phone interview.
7 Ibid.
8 Abeid.
9 Ibid.
10 Kissimmee, Joey (2016, June 16). Phone interview.
11 Cochrane, Todd (2016, May 23). Phone interview.
12 Ibid.
13 Campbell.
14 Martin, Shannon (2016, June 8). "Where should I host my podcast?" *Podcasting Blog*. [https://podcastingblog.com/2016/06/08/where-should-i-host-my-podcast/]
15 Ibid.
16 Walch, Robert (2016, May 23). Phone interview.
17 Ibid.
18 Ibid.
19 Ibid.
20 Ibid.
21 Ibid.
22 Ibid.
23 Cochrane.
24 Martin, Shannon (2016, July 6). Personal interview.
25 Ibid.
26 Ibid.
27 Ibid.
28 "Become a SoundCloud pro" (2016). *SoundCloud*. [https://soundcloud.com/pro]
29 Piazza, Anna (2016, July 7). Personal interview.
30 Ibid.
31 "Podcasts Connect help," *Apple*. [https://help.apple.com/itc/podcasts_connect/#/]
32 Thorpe, Shawn (2015, Mar. 27). "iTunes album art spec goes up again," *Podcaster News*. [http://podcasternews.com/2015/03/27/itunes-album-art-spec-goes-up-again/]

8

Growing and Sustaining Your Podcast

Now that your podcast is on iTunes, you may wonder: Where are the 10,000 downloads? Where are all the people "liking" your episode and saying how funny and great you are? All that work and just a handful of downloads. What gives?

"Saying 'I'm going to get famous by being on iTunes' is like saying 'I'm going to be famous because I'm in the phonebook,'" said David Jackson, founder of the School of Podcasting. "Because that's all it is—it's a giant phonebook of podcasts."[1]

Remember, Apple announced in 2013 that podcast subscriptions on iTunes surpassed 1 billion, with 250,000 unique podcasts available in 100 different languages.[2] All 250,000 of those podcasts are competing with each other to get noticed. What makes yours so special?

Just showing up does not get you an audience. Don't get me wrong: You've achieved a great deal. You've planned, recorded, edited and posted your first podcast. Hours', more likely days' worth of effort. That's an achievement of which to be proud. But instant success in podcasting is a rare, maybe an impossible, thing without some help.

Take *Serial*, for example. All the news reports about this breakout hit might give the impression it suddenly appeared out of nowhere. But, the show was a spinoff of "This American Life," the popular weekly public media radio show and podcast. The first episode of *Serial*, in fact, aired on "This American Life." Right from the start, it had a leg-up to success. Unless you have a built-in audience, celebrity status or a similar platform from which to launch, your audience is going to be small at the start.

But that's OK. The key to growing your podcast is to grow your audience.

John Siuntres started the *Word Balloon* podcast in 2005, before there was any social media to speak of. He compared his early grassroots efforts in audience cultivation to Johnny Appleseed, connecting to one listener at a time. Visiting comic-book-fan message boards, he'd introduce himself, share a link to his podcast and move on.

> Slowly, I was able to build this audience and also, because of live events like comic-book conventions, I would do my interviews live at the conventions and go up to tables and talk to the creators. But even more so, I was being invited to moderate panels for these creators on various subjects and again having a live audience. "Hi, I'm John Siuntres. I'm from the *Word Balloon* podcast," I would explain. "I do these interviews. If you want to hear more conversation like what we're about to hear today at this panel, come to my website." And yeah, it just slowly grew.[3]

Growing your audience goes back to the beginning steps of creating a podcast. Jackson said:

> You have to figure out who your audience is and then you have to make something that they want to hear. You have to go where they are. You can't do this from your chair unless you're going to a Google group or a Facebook group or whatever. But you need to connect with your audience. Usually, you do that before you record your podcast, because how are you going to know what to record about unless you know your audience?[4]

All through the planning and production of your first episode, you should've been asking yourself, "Who am I making this podcast for?" The answer should've informed all of your decisions about content and format. If you didn't do that, if you were only producing the podcast for yourself, then the scope of your podcast will be quite small.

That's fine. But if you want people to hear what you've got to say, you've got to listen and learn what interests them. Jackson said:

> Make friends. Build relationships. Why? Because the next step is [to] tell them about your podcast. Well, if you skipped that step of making relationships and making friends—if you just walk in and say, "Oh my gosh, this is my target audience. Hi, I'm Dave. You guys should listen to my podcast." They go, "Who is this person, and how do we get this spammer out of this group?"[5]

That's what happened to Jackson back in the days before Facebook.

> There were bulletin boards, and I walked into a forum built for ex-deejays. I walked in and said, "Oh, I'm Dave Jackson from the School of Podcasting. You guys should all start podcasts." Banned instantly, because I had no relationship with these people. Why would they listen to me? They didn't know who I was. So you've got to build relationships. Then tell them about your podcast. It's one of those things. The more personal you can do it, the better the outcome. Face to face is much better than Skype to Skype or phone to phone, but phone to phone is better than email to email because now I've got tone of

FIGURE 8.1 David Jackson is the host of *The School of Podcasting.*

voice. . . . That's how you grow your audience. A lot of people, they get into iTunes and they're waiting for Jimmy Fallon to call so they can go on "The Tonight Show," and it just doesn't work that way.[6]

Making friends, either online or in person, not only grows your audience, it helps you identify potential guests and topics for upcoming episodes. These new friends can also become channels to get your message out to all of their friends and followers.

"One of the best things about doing a seven-day-a-week podcast, when you're interviewing successful entrepreneurs, is that you're interviewing successful entrepreneurs and they have big audiences," said John Lee Dumas, host of *EOFire*.

So every single day, my first email was to my guest whose interview just went live and I say: "Tim Ferriss, Barbara Corcoran, Gary Vaynerchuk, your interview just went live on *EOFire*. Here [are] all the links to share your great story with your audience if you so choose—I'd be honored. Thanks a lot for being on the show." And when they do, then my podcast is getting exposed to a huge audience every single day, some of whom are becoming listeners, subscribers and potentially evangelists.[7]

Speaking of evangelists, what about reaching out to people who are evangelists for the medium already—your fellow podcasters? They've got an audience that likes to listen to podcasts. Maybe that audience would like to listen to your podcast.

"I think there are opportunities to promote other podcasts, to appear on other podcasts and build out a community, whether that's on Facebook or Twitter or other locations, Instagram, et cetera, where you're engaging that community. So, often, people listen to a podcast and in some ways it feels very one-way but yet it's also very intimate," said Brendan Monaghan, CEO of Panoply.

It's in your ears, physically in your body, and you're taking that voice in. And so there's an intimate kind of connection there, and I think fans and listeners love to have that two-way connection, whether it's on Facebook or Twitter or some other way to communicate with this voice that's off in the ether.[8]

GET SOCIAL ON SOCIAL MEDIA

Fortunately for beginning podcasters, one of the best promotional tools around is at your fingertips—and it's free.

"Social media is a definite smart move," said Cheryl Tan, host of STAND-OUT with Cheryl Tan.

> It's critical, to be honest. I've got a lot of listens through Twitter, from social media. I think what it is is explaining the value to any potential listeners on social media and then sending them back to your show.[9]

Hosts Ann Friedman and Aminatou Sow already had well-developed social media presences when they launched *Call Your Girlfriend*. Prolific tweeters, they were comfortable sharing information about the podcast and voicing why it was important for listeners to follow them online. It wasn't a one-way street, though; they were engaging their audience in a dialogue, which was key.

"If someone is coming from the realm of broadcasting, they may be accustomed to this sort of promotional strategy that feels very 'From me, the producer, to all you listeners out there,' but [try] to have a conversation [with your audience, instead]—to really kind of embody the voice of whatever project you're on," Gina Delvac, producer of Call Your Girlfriend, said.[10]

Call Your Girlfriend is "loose and conversational," which makes it a great fit for promoting on social media, according to Delvac. But, Twitter and Facebook posts shouldn't just be about the latest episode or event announcement. "[To] post a funny picture or post an article that's relevant to your sub-area or to engage in the voice about the podcast with other prominent people in that arena is hugely helpful," she said.

Tan warns warns against relying on your personal Facebook page alone to promote your podcast. Friends and family may appreciate your efforts, but they're not going to be the target audience you seek.

> What I would do instead is if, for example, you have a business podcast, create some really great headlines and then photos that go with it on Twitter that explain the value of your content to your audience.

That's the bottom line. You can use Twitter as well as LinkedIn. I've heard people have really good success on Pinterest actually, because it's such a very visual medium. Create an image. I'm big on quotes, so I'll pull out quotes and put them on boards and connect that to that podcast episode. It ties people back to your website. I'm a big believer in tying it to your website over iTunes. That's just me, because on my website is where people will sign up for my list. If they want to become a media magnate, they're going to sign up for that list on my website.[11]

MAKE A MARKETING PLAN

Tan's marketing advice for podcasters is simple. "If you are thinking about a podcast today, think about marketing yesterday, because it needs to happen," she said. "The marketing process—all it is is letting people know what you're doing, so that they can find you, listen to you, love you. That has to happen right away."[12]

Tan, never intended to start a podcast. But, with 20 years as a TV broadcaster under her belt, and with experience interviewing business professionals on the "Hampton Roads Business Weekly" show, she thought she knew enough about marketing to give a presentation at the 2015 DC PodFest to teach podcasters how they could get the media to notice them.

I knew that I was going to be speaking there on media, and I knew I'd be talking to podcasters. So it was like, "You know, I really should think about getting in the space, so I can understand where podcasters live and who they are and what they are trying to do and how it's going to help their business. I should probably do it myself first."[13]

Her first step was to develop "Get Media Smart," a two-week challenge, as a lead magnet.

That is something that when you're either at the top of your show or on your website, if you're creating a blog as well, you let people know: "Hey, you know my show's notes are on my website at cheryltanmedia.com. While you're there, take a look at this free guide that I've created for you or this free challenge." And in my case, it was Two Weeks to Become a Media Magnet. "Go ahead and download that, I've got a PDF guide for you to stay connected." It's totally about creating that

FIGURE 8.2 Cheryl Tan is a television broadcaster who hosts *STANDOUT with Cheryl Tan.*

> relationship. . . . This is something free, a free gift for somebody who can stay connected with me. That way I can connect with them and email them and let them know when new stuff was happening.[14]

After those initial two weeks, she decided to continue doing interviews as a podcast.

> I only intended that first two weeks to be kind of a lead magnet, to get people on my list, and that was fine. But then I really began to like it. When I thought about "Who do I want to reach? Who do I want to talk to? How do I want to create this other show that can be completely different from 'Get Media Smart' and be what I want it to be?" And that's where I came out with STANDOUT.[15]

According to Tan, getting people to notice your podcast ties into the reason why you are creating this content in the first place.

> Let's say you're a beer brewer and you want to podcast about brewing beer. People likely know that you are a brewer and you love it. Maybe

a month before your podcast starts, raise some red flags. "Hey, we're starting a podcast on beer brewing," and your audience is automatically going to love that.[16]

Even before you start your podcast, it's important to identify your potential audience and establish a relationship with them right away.

> The thing I think that people may not be doing is they're not creating a list to collect emails or a way to collect emails before their podcast starts. Podcasts are great for getting attention for who you are and what we do. But you want them to have an opportunity to connect deeper with you. They're not necessarily going to convert the client right away, if you don't give [the client] a chance.[17]

Create a platform for interacting with your audience. Social media is great for that, but you should also leverage the power of your website as a meeting place, where your audience members can learn more about you and share information about themselves. Add a message board or an email signup list so you can send updates and announcements.

> Maybe you tell them to join a Facebook group that you started just for your podcast. Maybe have them go back to your website and download a free guide that helps them brew better beer or six steps to making more money with your podcast, that kind of thing. Have them come back to your home, and just start building that email list. That email list will be a way for you to say to those people, "Hey, we've got a new episode coming up. We're interviewing so-and-so on the types of hops you need for your new beers to taste great" or whatever that is.[18]

Engendering that kind of rapport has to happen before you even post your first podcast, in order to create awareness among your potential audience and foster anticipation for your content.

Tom Tate is product marketing manager for AWeber Email Marketing, which, as the name might suggest, helps businesses promote their goods or services through email campaigns. He said email marketing is a great way for podcasters to grow their audience.

> I really love to advocate email as a tool to send a one-to-one email to an individual. That person might be reading it with a cup of coffee in

the morning. That person might be on the train. Really, think about your subscriber and send them relevant, engaging content that's going to allow you to build a stronger relationship with them. One of the things that you don't necessarily get with podcasting is that feedback loop, because you're pushing out content or you're not always getting people you know responding back or engaging with you. I think with email, you can definitely start to see that.[19]

While Tate appreciates social media and the dialogue it can create, he said that email is often better at reaching its target.

With Facebook and Twitter—[and] now with Instagram—a lot of that is algorithmic based, and you're subject to any changes in those algorithms. If you're a business or a podcaster and you push out content on Facebook through a Facebook page, the visibility of your content is going to be subject to change based on any changes in that Facebook algorithm. That's why you'll see a lot of times, if you want to get additional exposure or an additional reach, you're going to have to pay for promotion of your content or you're gonna have to pay for ads on those platforms.[20]

That means spending money on Facebook or Twitter ads.

With email, you're not really subject to all those algorithms, so when you send an email, if you're sending it with an email service provider that has strong deliverability, it's going to go to that person's inbox and it's going to show up ranked just like every other email that person is going to receive. Your likelihood that somebody is going to actually open and engage that content is going to increase. So it's a really great, viable way to send permission-based messaging to people who actually want to hear from you.

To be successful, the email should contain more than just news about an upcoming episode. It should include something unique that only subscribers can access. Think of it as a special club where members receive an extra 20 minutes of audio or premium content. This not only rewards people who have already subscribed, it entices others to do the same.

What you'll see is that your most engaged listeners will follow through with that, and you're going to start to slowly build a list of people who not only want your content but want to hear from you and then you can continue to send them news about your show.[21]

Email is not just a one-way street either. It can be a vehicle for learning more about your audience and thereby enriching the content of your podcast.

> I think a lot of people think about marketing and they think it's all pushing notifications and pushing your messaging, but [email is] a really great way to send out a quick one-question survey. If you have a list of 100 people and you say, "Hey, who would you like to see on the show, or what topics would you like me to talk about?" And only 10 people get back to you, [that's a] 10 percent response rate, which isn't that bad. You're going to get some valuable information about what you can do to better serve your audience, and you're going to get that from really engaged listeners.[22]

Developing an email list can be beneficial in other ways. If you have 10,000 total listeners and half of them subscribe to your email newsletter, you can tell a potential advertiser that 5,000 listeners are super-engaged with your podcast and could be interested in what that business is advertising. Likewise, if you want to sell a product, you've got a base of people to market that product to.

> It's a great asset to have for marketing purposes. But it's really just a great way to continue to drive people back to your new episodes, to again ask questions, ask people what they want to hear, who they want to see on the show. It's just a great way to have more of a two-way interaction with your listeners than with the podcast. There are times where I feel like I'm creating content, I'm pushing it out and I'm never sure how the audience is reacting or responding to that specific episode. But with email, you would be surprised at the amount of times that people will hit the reply button and actually send you a message back, either to affirm or to counter what you might have written.[23]

Another thing to understand about promotion is that doing a podcast might not be newsworthy enough for media outlets to notice. If Beyoncé starts a podcast, Tan said, that's news. But, another podcast of two people talking about movies probably isn't.

> But, if you are an expert in your field and you're starting a podcast, you're leading with your expertise and not the fact that you have a podcast. The fact that you are talking in the media about what your expertise is—you can let people then know that you do have a podcast, and they'll find you that way.[24]

Tan described two strategies for podcasters who want to get their podcast noticed by the media. The first is targeting outlets that might be interested in your expertise.

> Let's go back to that beer brewer. That beer brewer who has just started a new kind of beer that is getting a lot of traction. Actually, beer brewers are kind of big business, and a lot of business stories are being written about them right now. There's a lot of attention being focused on them. To me, if I'm a beer brewer and I'm getting a following, I would go to my local news—I love local, by the way, I'm a big believer in starting with local media and working your way up. Find a food editor for a local newspaper and talk about your brand-new beer, the brand-new concoction you're creating and how you're getting buzz from the local beer-loving community.[25]

In that feature, the brewer will talk about starting the brewery, why he loves beer and, did you know, he has a podcast about brewing?

> The media attention can bring attention to your podcast, even though you didn't say, "Hi, I'm a podcaster on beer." You led with your beer-brewing experience, love, hops and all of that kind of thing, but targeting the right person. If you had sent that pitch to the health reporter? Probably not as effective as [sending it] to the food reporter at your local paper.[26]

The second strategy Tan described was creating an event around your subject that news outlets might be interested in covering.

> Let's say you have a big day and you're testing out some new hops. I don't really know anything about beer brewing, but if you're testing out something brand new and you're willing to have a TV station come in and test out the concoction with you and see the process inside, give a special tour of the inside of your brewery, then you're giving them an exclusive into your world and, "Oh hey, I'm starting the podcast, because people love talking about the best ways to make beer." And I'm pretty sure that reporter will talk about that, because it's interesting. That's attention to your podcast. I think media attention definitely has a goal, as mainstream journalists are fascinated right now by podcasts, but at the end of the day, they don't want to focus on your podcast. They want to focus on your expertise. If you can share that expertise and talk about your podcast, I think you can get a win-win for everybody.[27]

HOW BIG IS YOUR AUDIENCE?

One of the most valuable tools podcast hosting companies provide for podcasters looking to grow their audience is reliable data analytics. These measurements not only tell you how many downloads you have, but, depending on the service, they can provide insights into who your audience is.

"I think the analytics and the metrics in this space are evolving right now," said Panoply's Brendan Monaghan.

> The download is the commonly used term, and it's something that frankly even within the industry, you can't find a common definition that a lot of companies agree upon, as simple as that might sound. I think the industry needs to have more transparency both in metrics but also in user behavior.[28]

Compared to television and radio, podcasting is still a relatively young medium, and coming to terms with how audience size is measured is one of the big debates going on within the industry.

> Radio is a $15 billion to $17 billion market, and podcasting, depending on who you talk to, was a $50 million to $200 million industry last year. There's a lot of room to run. There's a lot of opportunity there, but there's also a lot of challenges to make podcasting a mainstream media platform.[29]

Accurate audience measurement would help podcasters and advertisers better understand listener engagement and help them calculate their return on investment. With an accurate accounting of audience size, a podcaster can more successfully negotiate with potential advertisers. Likewise, if an ad buyer is going to spend X number of dollars on a podcasting commercial, they want assurance it's going to reach the audience the podcaster is promising.

> In general, I think there's a lot of benefit both to the editorial folks as well as the salespeople to have more insight into listenership. One thing that we've done is we've got our own branded player that shows can embed on their website. That's a step shy of having our own podcast app, but it does give us insight into how far people listen and what they're listening to and what their behavior is like.

This is the crux of the podcast measurement problem. Is a download an accurate measurement of listener engagement? Someone may download an episode but decide not to listen to it. Some might argue that the act of downloading is a form of engagement: The listener made a choice to download that episode. But even that's problematic, when you consider many people use podcatchers that automatically download episodes. How do you measure engagement in that scenario?

"We're at a point now where podcast measurement is evolving, and it's evolving to be more mature like website metrics have evolved," said Steve Mulder, senior director of audience insights at NPR.[30]

In the world of websites, audience is measured in three ways. "There's a company's internal metrics. Google Analytics is the classic example of an internal, complete, comprehensive number of records and deep-dive analytics on your own website," Mulder said.

That's one source. The second source is typically for advertising, so you get ad providers like DoubleClick, providing optimized metrics on ad delivery, viewability, views and so forth. And it's a different data

FIGURE 8.3 Steve Mulder is senior director of audience insights at NPR.

source, but it's specifically tailored for measuring ads and sponsorship, so that totally makes sense.[31]

The third source of data is competitive metrics, which are supplied by a third-party source and show how well your podcast performs against others.

> When you want to look at "How is my side doing against somebody else?" you need like an objective Switzerland who can help to look at that. So comScore and Nielsen are fantastic sources for doing this, because you can get data comparing different properties and they're compared in a very apples-to-apples way so that anybody looking at that can feel confident that they're getting a nice comparison data. And it's useful and it's accurate. The world of podcast is now falling into place with those same three kinds of data sources.[32]

In the first category, large organizations like NPR are able to generate detailed, Google Analytics–type data around the content they produce.

> Every time an audio player or web browser is trying to listen to or download a podcast, they're asking the server hosting that podcast, "Give me that file," and the CDN (content delivery network) says, "Here you go. Here's the file." It writes that request to a log file and then what we can do on a daily, weekly and constant basis is look through all those . . . millions of log file entries. From that, [we can] generate the numbers to identify how many people downloaded, what did they download, how many downloads and kind of run the math and effectively generate metrics based on those raw log files.[33]

This is the data that podcast hosting providers and many organizations are able to provide to their users.

In the second category, ad servers act as a third-party service within the podcasting space to deliver numbers on ad performance on podcasts, which is exactly the information advertisers want.

> The third category around podcasts is emerging still. But it's more competitive comparison data on podcasts. For years, iTunes, Apple, was really the only source of comparative data. And honestly it wasn't all that useful, because the ranker that iTunes uses, the Top Podcasts in Apple, was always a little unclear about how this [was] calculated.

It seemed to be more of like a top 20 list or a top 10 list of what was changing and hot right now versus a true definitive "by number of downloads, here's the top list."[34]

Other sources are beginning to pop up to fill this need for comparative data. Podtrac, for example, recently began to publish monthly rankings of all major podcast producers.

Pretty much everybody's in there now, and their approach is much more strict in terms of [being] based on actual audience size and measured in a consistent way, and it's a new entry into the field. Podtrac's been around for a while, but this idea of a published ranker that everyone can look at is a new idea and a much needed one as well. So you've got those three sources of data, and we use all three of those at NPR.[35]

WHY NOT MAKE SOME MONEY WITH YOUR PODCAST?

Even as the industry hammers out the definition of what constitutes listener engagement, enough data already exists to encourage networks like Acast, Midroll, Panoply and PodcastOne to get behind podcast advertising in a big way.

What those networks have discovered is that podcasting's greatest strength as an advertising vehicle lies in the intimate relationship between the podcast host and the audience. At Midroll, for example, all the commercials are host-read ads aimed at leveraging that relationship.

"Almost all of the hosts have used the product or service, whether it was a free sample or whether it's something that they already used," said Dan Franks, business manager at Midroll Media and co-founder/co-organizer of Podcast Movement. "It's something that they can speak on with some legitimacy, and they're not just reading ad copy for something that they're not familiar with. It's something that they've had some experience using."[36]

The networks are relying on dynamic insertion to place ads—host-read or pre-recorded commercials—in the beginning (pre-roll), middle (mid-roll) or end (post-roll) of a podcast episode. This process allows them to swap out new ads whenever they need to, rather than having an ad exist as part of the actual audio file.

"You can have Ford and Lexus simultaneously—running at the same time," said Sarah van Mosel, Acast's chief commercial officer.

> When you push play on your app, you'll hear a Ford ad, and when I push play on mine, I'll hear a Lexus ad, but they'll never run next to each other in an ad break. What we're doing is we're rotating through.[37]

If a podcast has 100,000 impressions a week, for example, and Ford and Lexus have each purchased 20 percent of those impressions, that leaves 60,000 impressions for Acast to sell to other advertisers.

> Whether it's one person that buys the other 60 percent or three other people that buy 20 percent [each], they're all rotating at the same time over the same period of time, because at any point the algorithm in the ad tech can determine "Whose ad should I run right now based on the variables? Is it a geotargeted campaign?" Is this request coming from Washington, DC? I have a campaign that can only run in Washington, DC, so I'm going to run that one for this request. It could be, is this campaign ending soon and I'm tracking behind? Maybe I should serve a whole bunch more of those so that it meets its goal. It's a complicated set of algorithms, as would be the case with serving display ads for a website or video ads for YouTube. There's lots of consideration [that goes into] deciding which ad to run during the same time period.[38]

Networks are able to sell advertising across their full slate of programming or to target specific podcasts to reach a desired audience.

> We have different benchmarks internally to determine what shows are good fits for us to work with. There's not really a number that we can just blast out and say, "Hey, if you're getting over this many downloads, then you're a good fit." It has a lot to do with the frequency that shows are published.[39]

But audience size is not necessarily the only consideration for the network or advertiser.

> If a show gets a smaller number of downloads, but they're published daily or five times a week or something like that, then maybe that is

more appealing to an advertiser, because they can sponsor a week's worth of shows versus a monthly show. That show needs to get a lot of listeners to get some legs out of those advertisements. While there is certainly a benchmark that we internally have that determines that shows are good to work with or not, there's a lot of variables.[40]

Unique content or genre can also play a factor in making a podcast attractive to a potential advertiser.

A lot of times, there are business podcasts where the people who are listening to the podcast are more likely to trust the host on the products or services they recommend. Since they're more likely to convert than maybe somebody that's passively listening to the podcast, because those businesspeople are actively looking to grow their business or learning how to get into business for themselves, those products or services are more likely to be purchased or acted on. Maybe [for] those types of shows we can deal with a little lower number in listenership versus some of the more passive listens to shows, where those might have higher numbers.[41]

It's fair to say that networks give audience size a great deal of weight in determining which podcasts they want to bring into the fold. But who that audience is can also factor into the decision-making process.

According to van Mosel, Acast's content strategy has been not to just go after "the usual suspects." In expanding to the U.S., the Swedish-based network has courted podcasts made by and targeting women of color and members of the LGBT community as a way to broaden its base.[42]

Even without huge audiences, new podcasters can find a way into some of these networks, provided they can bring in unique content or a different type of audience. Still, there are opportunities outside of networks for a podcaster to make money through advertising and other means.

Adam Sachs, former CEO at Midroll, says that one of the problems many new podcasters make is they try to monetize too early.

I think that we have seen in our conversations with advertisers that there's a certain threshold, for the most part—an audience number that an advertiser wants to see before they'll want to pay to advertise on a podcast episode. That number can vary depending on what kind of show it is.[43]

For example, if someone is producing a podcast for iOS developers, that might be the ideal podcast for a technology advertiser who's looking for a focused, high-quality listener who's interested in iOS development.

> An advertiser knows exactly what they're getting. They know that these people are tech savvy. They spend money, whatever it is, so the threshold for minimum listeners for a show like that is a lot smaller than, say, the threshold for your run-of-the-mill comedy interview podcast, of which there are now many and of which the audience could be very varied, very diverse. It's a lot harder to really understand, for that advertiser, exactly who they're getting when they advertise on that show.[44]

If as a beginning podcaster, you have chosen the right topic and are targeting the right audience, opportunities may exist for selling advertising or sponsorships. Reach out to vendors who may want to advertise to the audience to whom you're catering.

EXPLORE MULTIPLE MODELS OF MONETIZATION

Few podcasters are as transparent about their monetization success as *EOFire's* John Lee Dumas. By visiting eofire.com/income, you can access all of the podcast's monthly income reports since 2012.

> We shared all of our revenue, all of our expenses, every single way that we monetize, because we really want to be that beacon of guidance for podcasters of like, "Hey, this is working. So this is what was working for us, so you can model that success." Also, this is what's not working, because a lot more things don't work for us than work for us, so they can avoid those failures.[45]

Some of Dumas' top ways of making money through his podcast are the goods and services he provides. He has a book called "The Freedom Journal," which teaches readers how to grow and make money off podcasting. He also offers Podcasters Paradise, step-by-step tutorials on the same subject.

> I use the podcast to drive traffic to that and to generate revenue. We have sponsors on the show. Another great thing about doing 30 episodes

a month is that I have sponsors that have a total of 60 spots, because I have two sponsors per episode. So now I have 60 sponsors essentially paying for 60 spots—or, more likely, it's more like 10 sponsors grabbing six spots each. That is another great way to monetize.[46]

EOFire also makes commissions from affiliates by recommending their products and services on the show.

While Dumas is pleased with his current success, he admitted that for the first six months of the podcast, he didn't see a dime.

At the seven-month point, I had a guy reach out to me who was a sponsorship broker and he said: "John, I've been brokering sponsors for a comedy podcast for years. We want to check out if it would be profitable to do the same thing for a business podcast." And the next thing I knew, I had my entire next month booked out for $12,000, and I said, "Oh wow, I'm actually going to make money."[47]

Jay Jacksonrao's love of geek culture inspired him to launch *The Nerdpocalypse,* as well as a string of pop culture–themed podcasts. Eventually, he turned that into his own network, TNP Studios. His recipe for monetization success was to put some of his podcasts behind a paywall.

We started the paywall in January 2015, and that's been going steadily very well. That's $5 a month or $50 for the full year. You get access to all of those shows. Across our network, we have over 100,000 monthly listeners. That's a pretty good place to get for several different niche podcasts.[48]

It's the niche nature of Jacksonrao's content that he credits for his network's success.

I think that the entire appeal of podcasts is to get exactly what you want when you want it. I think when you're starting a podcast it's very easy to say, "Well, I'm going to do a show that is going to be on this really broad topic because then I'll have more people [listening]." But the problem is you are a very, very small fish in an ocean trying to somehow get attention, which is damn near impossible. However, if you decide "I'm going to do this thing, this specific topic," especially if the topic is not something that a lot of people were hitting on, [something that] people have an interest in, then you become the absolute big fish in this incredibly small pond.[49]

Listeners can sign up for TNP Studios' premiere content via a banner ad on the network's website, which will take them to the signup page.

> Once you sign up, you're redirected to PayPal and you come back and you create your login and what have you into our website. We have it set up so that we post much like any of our other posts. Everyone can see those posts, whether you're a fan or not. When you go to sort of click on "read more" to go listen, if you're not a premium member or not logged in, it'll tell you: "Hey, you can access this content. Here's how you sign up." But if you're signed in as a premium member and you click "read more," you can listen to it right there or you can subscribe using an RSS feed, so that it will show up being like iTunes or you can do it on your phone so there's a certain password and user name that's associated with it.[50]

In many ways, Jacksonrao's approach has the best of both worlds. The niche nature of his podcasts allows him to target specific topics and audiences, but as a network, he can cross-promote from show to show.

Mark Glaser is executive editor and founder of MediaShift and Idea Lab. He raises money through sponsorships from companies like Squarespace and GoDaddy. He also supplements that financing through in-person training events.

> We've done one-day Collabspace events, and they're basically an all-day event where we have startups present and we work together using kind-of improv comedy techniques to get people to work together and help the startups succeed. We also have done weekend hackathons for journalism school students, and some of them have been women hackathons and some of them have been coed at journalism schools, or it's a weekend hackathon and kind of a startup weekend where they have to come up with startup ideas and pitch them to the judges.[51]

Glaser and his colleagues use their digital media expertise via online training courses or in partnerships with universities. "They provide the instructors," he said. "We do one-hour trainings to help people with digital skills,

FIGURE 8.4   Mark Glaser is executive editor and founder of MediaShift and the Idea Lab.

like social media or shooting video or audio or how to launch a podcast or Snapchat for journalists. We do them in partnership with schools or people in our community if contributors can do trainings."[52]

While Glaser doesn't make money directly from the *MediaShift* podcast, it serves as a promotional platform for the training his team offers. The podcast is not the direct moneymaking feature; rather, it's a piece of the whole MediaShift puzzle.

> We charge typically $39 for a training, and . . . if the podcast helps us refer someone to a training and they end up signing up for it, then we make money from that. Or an event like Collabspace, where we

charge $99 for people to come, and they pay for it, then we're basically making income that way.[53]

Bill McKenna of *Not Another Podcast?* also hosts events like monthly meet-ups at a local bar, but those are mostly an opportunity to generate some audience engagement.

"We do a thing called 'Pod Crawl,' which is a podcast bar crawl the second Saturday in September," he said. "The first year we did it, we had about 150 people, and last year we had about 300 show up."[54]

Where McKenna makes money is the *Not Another Podcast?* online store, where fans can buy stickers, baseball caps and Pod Crawl T-shirts. You can even host a live show for $3,000.

McKenna also raises money through two programs that are good fits for podcasters just starting out in the moneymaking game.

First is the Amazon Associates Program [https://affiliate-program.amazon.com/welcome]. Basically, this puts an online store on your website, which you can customize around specific products of interest to your listeners. Got a golf podcast? Choose a set of golf clubs your audience might crave from the Amazon store, and that becomes a custom ad on your website. Amazon will pay you a percentage of the price of every item sold from your website.

When it comes to accepting donations from PayPal [www.paypal.com], think of it as a tip jar at your local coffee shop. Once you set up an account and add a button on your website, ask your audience to support your show by donating whatever amount they see fit.

Accepting donations is a form of crowdfunding, which can be a great way to finance your podcast. Crowdfunding platforms like GoFundMe [www.gofundme.com], Indiegogo [www.indiegogo.com] and Kickstarter [www.kickstarter.com] have helped provide startup money for movies, book projects, new technology and, yes, podcasts.

Patreon [www.patreon.com] takes a slightly different approach to soliciting support from listeners. Rather than raising money around one-time campaigns like Kickstarter or Indiegogo, Patreon provides a platform for ongoing, sustaining support from regular donations.

"The number one thing you can do is just start the page," said Jordan Cope, Patreon's creator discovery manager.

> The fun thing about is Patreon is that we only take 5 percent of whatever you process. There are no fees for using the site, no fees for starting your campaign or anything like that. It's just 5 percent of whatever you bring in month after month.[55]

The trade-off to going the crowdfunding route is that you need to set up rewards for the various donation levels. For example, if someone donates $50, you may give them a shout-out on your podcast, or $500 might get them an appearance on mic.

BUILD A COMMUNITY AROUND PODCASTING

In many ways, crowdfunding and donations seem like apt forms of financing for a podcast, which is a medium focused on niche content and giving a platform to voices that aren't usually heard in mass media. It's a very from-the-bottom-up philosophy.

Soon after Adam Curry, one of podcasting's founders, launched *No Agenda* with co-host John C. Dvorak, he realized that it took a lot of effort to put out a daily podcast. They wouldn't be able to continue if the audience didn't chip in. So, they asked their listeners to send them whatever they thought the podcast was worth.

> It turns out that people put very different values [on it] based upon their own value system and their own capacity. They put very different values on a piece of programming. And we tuned in to that pretty early on. We created what we called the value-for-value system, whereas, OK, we just delivered a half hour, an hour, two hours, whatever it is of entertainment. If you enjoyed it, what is that worth to you? Did you go to the movies last night and you bought popcorn, a drink, [for] two people? Fifty bucks. So which is worth more? And by the way, if you don't want to give us anything, enjoy the show. No problem. And that caught on. People started to really show what they'd thought it was worth, and you have people who can just have a different idea about it.[56]

Some listeners contributed $4 a month or maybe, if they really liked an episode, $500. Others didn't have money to give but found other ways to show their support.

We discovered that people are not only willing to contribute value in the monetary sense but also in research, jingles, artwork, all kinds of production stuff. People jumped in and said, "Hey, you know, I'll run your servers. . . . I'll do it. It's worth it to me. I like it." And that just grew and grew and grew, and we started thanking people on the show and telling them this person gave us $50 and here's $5 this person [gave] and sometimes a little note, and we discovered that the network really is the network of people that are in it within the environment of this program.[57]

This was a new way of thinking, as far as Curry was concerned. It's one thing to have listeners call in and give feedback about a radio show; it's another thing for them to join in the making of the podcast.

But to have people actually creating little bits or recording things and just really acting as producers and sending information, that was something that was new, and the reason why is because they could do it. This was never really possible before.[58]

Podcasting is not broadcasting. It's a conversation. You formulate an idea, record and produce content and then send it out to the audience you've identified. You grow the podcast through promotion and listening—always listening—to what your listeners say. If they like what you're saying, they'll tell you and support you. If they don't, they'll tell you that too, or they won't listen at all, which is another kind of message. You post more podcasts. You listen more. Eventually, you're in a dialogue with your audience. What started as you talking into a microphone at your dining room table has become a whole online community built around something you came up with.

To build that community, to start that conversation, to begin to listen and grow, you have to podcast. What are you waiting for?

ACTIVITIES

1. All through the process of launching your podcast, you've been focusing on who your audience is. Even before your first episode is posted, come up with a promotional plan to engage your target audience. Use social media and word of mouth to send people to your website, encouraging them to sign up for email alerts. Make sure there's relevant content on your website, including your biography and an FAQ [frequently asked questions] section

describing the mission of your podcast and how people can get in contact with you. Consider creating a lead magnet—extra content to entice your audience to sign up for email and follow you on social media. As you post more episodes, continue to ask people to sign up for email alerts, so that you can begin building your email list for future promotions.

2. Establish social media accounts for your podcast on Twitter, Facebook and any other platform that your target audience uses. Don't go overboard: Two or three platforms should be enough to start. Promote every new podcast across all the platforms. After five or so episodes, evaluate which platform is bringing in the most traffic, and begin to shift the balance of your attention there. Interact with your audience on social media. Don't just "blast out" announcements about new episodes. Ask them questions. Thank them for liking your post or for following you. Start having a dialogue with your audience, and solicit their feedback on how to make the podcast better.

3. The first step in putting together a monetization plan is to figure out how much you're spending to produce a podcast episode. Put a dollar figure on how many hours you put into the production of an episode; add in how much you pay in hosting fees for your website and audio hosting service per episode. You've already purchased equipment (microphones, recorder, etc.) for your launch. These are startup expenses, so they can be divided over the total number of episodes you plan to do. Once you've added any extraneous fees to this total, you've determined your "nut." This is how much each episode costs to produce. Then, use your data analytics to determine your audience size. If it's a big number (10,000+ listeners per episode), you may be able to sell advertising on your website or podcast. If you have a smaller, more niche audience, you may be able to target specialized advertising or sponsorships—amusement park discount tickets on a rollercoaster enthusiasts podcast, for example. For podcasts with smaller but loyal audiences, consider crowdfunding, donations or merchandise to subsidize your podcast. It may take a combination of approaches to finance your podcast.

NOTES

1 Jackson, David (2016, Aug. 6). Skype interview.
2 Friedman, Lex (2013, July 22). "Apple: One billion iTunes podcast subscriptions and counting," *Macworld*. [www.macworld.com/article/2044958/apple-one-billion-itunes-podcast-subscriptions-and-counting.html]
3 Siuntres, John (2016, June 18). Phone interview.
4 Jackson.

5 Ibid.
6 Ibid.
7 Dumas, John Lee (2016, July 14). Skype interview.
8 Monaghan, Brendan (2016, June 14). Phone interview.
9 Tan, Cheryl (2016, June 18). Skype interview.
10 Delvac, Gina (2016, July 11). Phone Interview.
11 Tan.
12 Ibid.
13 Ibid.
14 Ibid.
15 Ibid.
16 Ibid.
17 Ibid.
18 Ibid.
19 Tate, Tom (2016, July 6). Personal interview.
20 Ibid.
21 Ibid.
22 Ibid.
23 Ibid.
24 Tan.
25 Ibid.
26 Ibid.
27 Ibid.
28 Monaghan.
29 Ibid.
30 Mulder, Steve (2016, Aug. 3). Phone interview.
31 Ibid.
32 Ibid.
33 Ibid.
34 Ibid.
35 Ibid.
36 Franks, Dan (2016, Aug. 17). Phone interview.
37 Mosel, Sarah van (2016, May 31). Phone interview.
38 Ibid.
39 Franks.
40 Ibid.
41 Ibid.
42 Mosel, van.
43 Sachs, Adam (2016, Aug. 18). Phone interview.
44 Ibid.
45 Dumas.
46 Ibid.
47 Ibid.
48 Jacksonrao, Jay (2016, June 13). Skype interview.
49 Ibid.
50 Ibid.
51 Glaser, Mark (2016, May 24). Phone interview.

52 Ibid.
53 Ibid.
54 McKenna, Bill (2016, May 17). Phone interview.
55 Cope, Jordan (2016, July 7). Phone interview.
56 Curry, Adam (2016, Aug. 16). Phone interview.
57 Ibid.
58 Ibid.

Appendix A

Music Rights, Incorporation and Other Legal Considerations

Picking up a microphone and recording your first episode can be an exhilarating experience. For the first time, it feels like you can say anything you want. You're not governed by the rules of the Federal Communications Commission. This is podcasting, after all. You can shout profanity for all 60 minutes of your one-hour podcast if you want to.

The First Amendment guarantees freedom of speech, but podcasters need to understand that that freedom is not absolute.

FIGURE BM.1 Kevin Goldberg, a member of the law firm Fletcher, Heald and Hildreth, PLC, in Arlington, Virginia, is an attorney who specializes in intellectual property rights.

Kevin Goldberg, a member of the law firm Fletcher, Heald and Hildreth, PLC, in Arlington, Virginia, specializes in First Amendment, Freedom of Information Act and intellectual property issues. He says that podcasters have many of the same responsibilities journalists do when it comes to areas like libel, slander, invasion of privacy and copyright law.

> One obvious thing would be defamation. If you are a podcaster that is trying to do something that is news-oriented, then you would have all of the same issues that a blogger might have, that a newspaper might have, that a broadcaster or that a radio station might have. . . . You definitely have the same core concerns, and that also extends to copyright, that extends to invasion of privacy.[1]

Even someone like a radio sports reporter who starts a podcast may not understand the legal issues of going from one medium to another.

> If you come from a radio background, you've probably enjoyed the basic statutory licenses that allow you to play music with your broadcast. However, most of the statutory licenses, which offer you one-stop shopping in terms of using music, don't apply to podcasting, and that is the big issue.[2]

When giving presentations on starting a podcast, one of the questions I'm always asked is, "Can I use my favorite song as my theme music?" The simple answer is probably not.

> The first thing you have to understand about any song that you hear on the radio, on television, in a podcast, online, is that the song actually contains two different copyrighted works. One is called the musical work. The other is called the sound recording. The musical work is the underlying music and lyrics, sometimes called the composition. The sound recording is the fixed version you are hearing at that moment.

Let's say you want to use the Beatles' song "Yesterday" as the theme for your podcast. John Lennon and Paul McCartney originally wrote the song, but you want to use the version recorded by Marvin Gaye.

> The musical work, again the composition of the music and lyrics, was created and originally owned by Lennon and McCartney. Everyone

who wants to publicly perform that song in any way, whether it is someone creating their own CD, someone performing it on the radio, even people doing live versions of it, they all have to pay for the right to perform that musical work. The same is true for the sound recording as well—whether the person who is singing is also the songwriter; in effect, a singer-songwriter gets paid twice.[3]

In the scenario suggested, if a podcaster wanted to use Marvin Gaye's cover of "Yesterday," he'd have to pay for both Lennon and McCartney—or whoever owns the musical work rights now—and the person who owns the performance rights to Marvin Gaye's version.

If I am a radio station, if I am a podcaster, if I'm the Washington Wizards and I'm playing a song in the arena, I have to pay for the right to publicly perform both the musical work and the sound recording. If I'm a podcaster, I have to pay for the right to perform the musical work; I have to pay the songwriter. I also have to pay the creator of the sound recording; that's most likely the recording artist. Of course, it could be the music publishing company that has bought up the songwriter's rights, and it could be the record label that owns a version of the sound recording. But in essence, you have to pay two different people.[4]

Before you start thinking you've found a loophole, however, don't think that you can simply do your own cover version of "Yesterday" to avoid having to pay copyright royalties to anyone. In that situation, you still must pay royalties to the owner of the musical work.

Further complicating things, every different medium constitutes a different performance. If a radio station is live-streaming "Yesterday," it still has to pay Lennon and McCartney as well as the artist covering the song.

"It gets a little trickier with the sound recording," Goldberg said. "A radio station does not have to get permission or pay royalties for playing a sound recording over the air. This has been very controversial, but it is the law."[5]

In 1998, Congress updated the copyright law to require that anyone performing a sound recording via digital transmission (including over the internet or satellite radio) get permission and potentially pay royalties. This means that while a radio station does not have to get permission or pay for the right to play the sound recording of Gaye's "Yesterday" over the air, it does have to get permission to stream the song, even as an internet simulcast of the over-the-air broadcast.

This is in addition to the permissions that must be obtained by radio and television stations to perform the musical works over the air and through streaming. Those permissions are obtained from the performing rights organizations known as ASCAP, BMI and SESAC.

> Radio stations are allowed to play musical works over the air by signing a licensing agreement with ASCAP, BMI and SESAC, usually all of them because you really can't pick and choose whose works you use to the exclusion of others. These licenses are referred to as 'compulsory licenses' because the copyright owner has to let you perform the work and you have to abide by the conditions, including the rate that you're agreeing to pay.[6]

Currently, the statutory licenses that exist with regard to digital transmissions involving the internet apply only to non-interactive webcasting or streaming, which some radio stations and services like Pandora provide. Unfortunately, podcasting is considered interactive webcasting. Therefore podcasters don't have a statutory license to help them secure rights for performance of musical works and/or sound recordings in their podcasts.

> The statutory licenses are a way to simplify the process for media that are so pervasive that going to the individual copyright owners each time they play a song would be impossible. It would be destructive to both sides of that equation. It wouldn't benefit either the copyright owners or the copyright users.[7]

Honoring musical work and performance rights extends to all recordings you do as part of your podcast. This includes podcasts that feature "live" performances by musicians or bands.

Part of Goldberg's job is to provide releases for his client radio stations. He's had the opportunity to watch bands perform a few songs live on air. Some of these performances were also recorded and posted as podcasts.

> In that situation, if they come in to you as a recording artist, you need to be concerned about a few different things. Number one, if they're

playing a cover, then they can't give you the right to perform the musical work, and so you're exposed to liability there. You want to insist that they are only playing songs that they have written themselves.[8]

Even if musicians on your show say a song is their own, you have to ascertain whether they actually have the right to give permission for you to record it.

The recording artist may not always be the copyright owner. The label may own the copyright. The band itself may not be able to give you legal permission. Even if they can, you might need permission from all five people in the band. One person can't speak on behalf of all of them, because they're all co-owners in copyright. . . . Intellectual property is like when a husband and wife buy a house and they're considered joint owners of the house on the deed, right? In that instance, you'd need to get the permission of both of them to buy their house.[9]

Also, it's not enough that you tell the artists you're recording them for a podcast. They should sign a release so that you have their permission down on paper.

It's not hard to do a release, and a release is going to be very helpful. On that release, you want the signature of every band member, hopefully. It doesn't have to include massive legalese. It just has to be clear as to what you're getting. And this is important for another reason: You get only what they clearly give in terms of permission.[10]

Those terms must clearly state any plans for the recording beyond just posting it as a podcast episode. Perhaps you want to make it your theme music or include it on a "best of" CD later on. Those rights don't automatically transfer just because the artist agreed to perform on one episode of your podcast.

The bottom line is you don't own that musical composition or the performance. You don't own the rights to the song. Unless you have a written agreement with the rights holders that spells out the parameters that allow you to do certain things, you don't have the right to use that music, whether it was performed live in your studio or is a recording you played on your podcast. Period.

There are podcasting formats that skirt these rules somewhat, but they still have legal standards the podcaster needs to adhere to in order to avoid being held liable. Music review or scholarly podcasts, for example, routinely include excerpts of songs in order to examine their artistic merit. They are able to do this because they're taking advantage of "fair use," a concept covered by Section 107 of the Copyright Act.

Courts apply four factors in measuring whether something constitutes fair use, according to Goldberg. These factors don't all have to be met, and courts are very fluid in how much weight they give to each.

> What fair use tries to do is to equitably balance the interests of the copyright owners and creators and incentivize those people to continue to create versus the First Amendment interests and other societal interests in building on or using those copyrighted works. Fair use recognizes that if it's too easy to use someone's material or content without permission, [artists] aren't going to be incentivized to create in the future and that we need to attach an economic value into artistic works in some regard.[11]

The first factor when determining whether something constitutes fair use considers the nature of the use, which is where criticism, scholarly review and the First Amendment come into play. Society has an interest in promoting the evaluation of creative works. The critic, journalist or podcaster has a First Amendment right to review artistic works. But there are limits to the way the excerpt can be used.

"There's a difference between somebody printing an article in the newspaper or playing a song in some kind of criticism and then later using that same critical clip to make money—for instance, as a commercial," Goldberg said.[12]

Perhaps you have a music journalism podcast and you did a special episode following Prince's death that included clips of his music to enhance your coverage. That may be considered fair use. But, if you turn around and use clips from that episode to promote a Kickstarter campaign to raise money for your podcast, you've changed the nature of that work.

> Even if the original work was scholarly in nature, something like a scholarly article from a journal that you're quoting on your website, or a portion of a music theory journal or an entertainment law journal of some kind, and you quote something about music and copyright about Prince. That's probably OK. But if you're suddenly charging access to

your work, to your podcast, that may change things. Now we're commercializing this. And even though the original writer or speaker never expected to get paid, they probably don't want you to get paid for using this as entertainment. They don't want you free riding.[13]

The second factor is the nature of the original work. Most musical works and sound recordings are commercial in nature. Any authorized use is going to be viewed warily where the "fair use" defense is being raised.

The third fair use factor concerns the amount and substantiality of the excerpt being used. According to Goldberg, this standard is often misinterpreted in two ways.

Number one, there is absolutely no threshold limit distinguishing between the use that might be fair and not fair. I always hear people say, "Well, I thought there was a 30-second maximum and that using anything less than that is fair." No, that's not true at all. There is no hard and fast limit. Something could be five seconds and be too much; something else could be 40 seconds and not be too much. It kind of depends on the overall work.[14]

Someone could take three seconds of a hip-hop beat and loop it over and over again to create a new commercial song, which, according to Goldberg, may not be considered fair use.

"Imagine if you had something called *The Movie Spoiler Podcast*, and all you did was take the new movies that come out and take the five seconds where the twist in the movie is ruined," he said. In this case, it's not so much the length of time taken but the nature of the content that is not fair.[15]

The final factor, which Goldberg said receives a bit more weight than the others, is if the use negatively impacts an artist's ability to commercialize his or her own work.

This gets back to the essence of fair use: Are we incentivizing a person to want to create more, or are we stealing from them? Is your use going to help the person, or is it going to take away from the person? Are you going to send more eyeballs and earbuds to a music video? Or are people going to say, "Hey, great, now I've got a copy of this. I don't need to buy it."[16]

In the end, determining what constitutes fair use is very unpredictable, Goldberg said, and it's really just a defense. Whenever possible, get permission.

Despite the strictures of intellectual property rights, podcasters do have a few options that allow them to use music.

If you're an artist or know someone who is a musician, you could find someone to do a cover version of a particular song. In that instance, you'd still have to pay for the right to use the musical work, but you wouldn't have to pay a major recording artist or label for the right to use the sound recording. Better yet, you could employ musicians to write a theme or provide background music that they've composed. Assuming they perform it as well (or you can find someone to perform it for free), then you have permission from the owners of both the musical work and sound recording. You'd still want to have written permission from the artist to do that, but at least you wouldn't have to track down Marvin Gaye's family, John Lennon's family and Paul McCartney to get the OK for the Marvin Gaye version of "Yesterday" on your show.

You could also use songs and recordings that are in the public domain.

> That's not something that most podcasters are interested in, because public domain generally means the song is so old that it's no longer protected by copyright. And even if you do use a musical work that's in the public domain, remember that you need to get permission to use both the musical work and the sound recording, the latter of which may have been recorded relatively recently and may not be in the public domain.[17]

While it may be OK to use Beethoven's Fifth Symphony as your theme, you'd still have to get permission from the copyright holders of the London Symphony Orchestra's 2010 recording to use it on your podcast.

Another option is to use an online service like Creative Commons [https://creativecommons.org], Free Music Archive [http://freemusicarchive.org], Instant Music Now [www.instantmusicnow.com], Opuzz [www.opuzz.com] or NEO Sounds [www.neosounds.com] to license a piece of music.

Most of these sites offer simple licenses that delineate the parameters of how the composition and recording can be used. For example, a license may grant unlimited use in all circumstances, or there may be limits such as the composition and recording may be used only on free podcasts. Be sure you understand the scope of the license before signing it and using the audio on your podcast. It might not seem so important during those first few free episodes that the song can't be used for a commercial podcast. But if you put up a paywall or start charging for downloads, you may be violating the terms of the license.

Though this appendix is addressing music, the same principles apply to all forms of intellectual property. You should seek the creator's permission to use any artwork, photographs or text that you post on your website.

Typically, the posting should include proper credit (e.g., Photo by John Smith) and a link to the work on the creator's website, if possible. Ask each creator how he or she would like the credit to be worded, and use that.

More importantly, just because something appears online doesn't mean it's in the public domain. Artists don't lose their right to make money or reproduce a work if they've posted it online. For that matter, it may turn out that someone posted the artwork without the artist's permission. Always secure creators' permission—preferably in writing—before using their work on your website or in your audio.

In the end, as a podcaster you need to respect intellectual property rights. Not only is it the right—and legal—thing to do, *you're* a content creator as well. You should extend the same support and respect to your fellow artists' work that you would want for your own.

If, after doing everything correctly, you find yourself in a legal battle, hire a lawyer.

> You'd be shocked how often I see people who receive a letter from someone—even the most innocuous threat, just like an inquiry—and blow it off. If you receive a letter from a lawyer, do not try to handle it yourself. You'd be surprised how often the clients do that. I think you should hire a lawyer.[18]

Goldberg also suggested new podcasters brush up on media law and familiarize themselves with the basics.

> If something doesn't pass the smell test, you may want to hire a lawyer to answer that question for you. Consider it an investment rather than an expenditure, given that whatever amount you pay now to a lawyer might save you later in the future.[19]

Contacting a lawyer is exactly what Jay Jacksonrao of TNP Studio did when he decided it was time to form a limited liability corporation (LLC) for his podcast.

According to Jacksonrao, an LLC is like a regular corporation, an entity formed under state law in order to protect the personal assets of people conducting a business.

"The differences between the two lie in the way each is taxed, the amount of ongoing compliance with state oversight agencies, the flexibility or rigidity of the management structure and how easy it is to sell the business in the future," Goldberg said.[20]

The benefit of a corporation or LLC is that it shields owners and operators from personal liability in most cases.

> In the event that a lawsuit is filed for copyright infringement, for example, it is generally going to be filed against the corporation or LLC, not the individual. Creditors can only pursue the corporation's or LLC's assets to satisfy business debts, leaving things like your house, car, personal bank accounts, et cetera, safe. Sometimes potential investors will only do business with a corporation or an LLC, not an individual.[21]

Jacksonrao decided to form an LLC for a couple of reasons.

> One, we were accepting money outside of donations, which, I think— if you're going to start taking people's money and legitimately tracking taxes and what have you—if you're going to do it, do it right. Two, I wanted to make sure that we were set up for it. Nobody in my organization gets paid right now. It's all for charity right now. It's for the greater good of the business. But at some point, we're moving towards actually paying salaries and things like that. I want to make sure that those things are all legitimately set up.[22]

Forming an LLC or corporation is not that difficult a process, and it's something that anyone who is serious about doing an ongoing podcast should consider.

> Forming a corporation or LLC simply requires filing the proper paperwork with the relevant agency in your state—generally the Department

of State, but some states and the District of Columbia actually have a separate corporations division instead. This initial paperwork is generally not difficult to draft and file and tends to follow a standard template (that the state agency may actually post online). The more difficult issues come before and after filing this initial formation document.[23]

"You will have to weigh which legal entity, an LLC or a corporation, best fits your needs," Goldberg said. "If going the corporate route, you may also need to consider the type of corporation you want to be if there are multiple options available."[24]

You may also consider forming a nonprofit, sometimes called a not-for-profit. In that case, your state may require you to file a different type of formation document and you would have to apply to the IRS afterward to receive tax-exempt status, Goldberg said.

Bill McKenna also formed an LLC for *Not Another Podcast?*—mainly because he wanted to make sure his business was "protected legally".

> The first 10 or 15 episodes, I was more concerned about getting the episodes out and things of that nature. Once we started doing that— we started in June 2014, and I [incorporated] Not Another Podcast Productions, LLC, in October. If someone tried to sue us or if something happened, we would have a corporate entity that would protect us from something like that.[25]

McKenna, who lives in Virginia, used LegalZoom [www.legalzoom.com] to incorporate Not Another Podcast Productions in the state of Delaware.

"We deal with a law firm not only to set up the LLC, but also to handle contracts between TNP Studios as a business and the host of the shows to make sure everybody is protected and [everything is] aboveboard," Jacksonrao said.[26]

More Resources

Creative Commons—Podcasting Legal Guide
https://wiki.creativecommons.org/wiki/Podcasting_Legal_Guide

Electronic Frontier Foundation—Blogger's Rights
www.eff.org/bloggers/

IRS—Limited Liability Company (LLC)
www.irs.gov/businesses/small-businesses-self-employed/limited-liability-
company-llc

NOTES

1 Goldberg, Kevin (2016, June 2). Phone interview.
2 Ibid.
3 Ibid.
4 Ibid.
5 Ibid.
6 Ibid.
7 Ibid.
8 Ibid.
9 Ibid.
10 Ibid.
11 Ibid.
12 Ibid.
13 Ibid.
14 Ibid.
15 Ibid.
16 Ibid.
17 Ibid.
18 Ibid.
19 Ibid.
20 Goldberg, Kevin (2016, Oct. 27). Email interview.
21 Ibid.
22 Jacksonrao, Jay (2016, June 13). Skype interview.
23 Goldberg (email).
24 Ibid.
25 McKenna, Bill (2016, May 17). Phone interview.
26 Jacksonrao.

Appendix B
Shopping Guide

For someone with no experience recording digital audio, figuring out what equipment to buy can be pretty daunting. The best advice, as stated in Chapter 2, is to start with the basics, master each piece of technology and add new equipment as you become more confident.

While conducting interviews for this book, I asked some of the podcasters what equipment, software and services they used to produce and distribute their podcasts. Each had a different approach, and those differences are reflected in the variety of technology represented here.

The one big piece of technology absent from the list is a computer. In most cases, you'll need one. Since that will likely be the biggest expense, I'll leave it up to you to decide what works best.

This list is not meant to be an endorsement of any particular product; the internet is full of alternatives. Use this instead as a cheat sheet to get started.

Also, don't go overboard. Remember, you can record and post a podcast using just a smartphone, or you can build a professional studio with a big mixer, multiple condenser microphones and soundproof walls. What works best for you could be somewhere in the middle. Figure out what you need by asking a lot of questions and doing a little research. Oh, and have fun. This is supposed to be fun.

Audio Editing Software

Adobe Audition—www.adobe.com/products/audition.html
Adobe Premiere (Video Editor)—www.adobe.com/products/premiere.html
Audacity—www.audacityteam.org
Cubase—www.steinberg.net/en/products/cubase/start.html
Ferrite (Mobile)—www.wooji-juice.com/products/ferrite/
GarageBand—www.apple.com/mac/garageband/

Hindenburg—http://hindenburg.com
Pro Tools—www.avid.com/pro-tools
Sony Vegas Pro—www.sonycreativesoftware.com/vegaspro

Audio Interface

IK Multimedia iRig Pro Audio/MIDI Interface (iPhone/iPad)—www.ikmultimedia.com/products/irigpro/
M-Audio M-Track MKII Two-Channel USB Audio Interface with Waves Plugins—www.m-audio.com/products/view/m-track-mkii
PreSonus AudioBox iTwo (iPad)—www.presonus.com/products/Audio Box-iTwo-Studio

Digital Recorders

Tascam DR-40—http://tascam.com/product/dr-40/
Tascam DR-44WL—http://tascam.com
Tascam DR-60D—http://tascam.com/product/dr-60d/
Zoom H4n—www.zoom-na.com/products/field-video-recording/field-record ing/zoom-h4n-handy-recorder
Zoom H5—www.zoom-na.com/products/field-video-recording/field-record ing/zoom-h5-handy-recorder
Zoom H6—www.zoom-na.com/products/field-video-recording/field-record ing/h6-handy-recorder

Headphones

AKG K52 Closed-Back Headphones—www.akg.com/pro/p/k52
Sony MDR7506 Professional Large Diaphragm Headphones—www.sony.com

Microphones

Blue Snowball (Condenser)—www.bluemic.com/products/snowball/
Blue Yeti (Condenser)—www.bluemic.com/products/yeti/
Heil PR 40 Dynamic Studio Recording Microphone (Dynamic)—www.heilsound.com/pro/products/broadcast-microphones/pr-40
MXL 990 USB (Condenser)—www.mxlmics.com/microphones/900-series/990-USB/
Rode Procaster Broadcast Dynamic Vocal Microphone (Dynamic)—www.rode.com/microphones/procaster

Sennheiser e 835 (Dynamic)—https://en-us.sennheiser.com/live-perfor mance-microphone-vocal-stage-e-835
Studio Projects B1—www.studioprojects.com/b1.html

Mixers

Behringer Xenyx 1204 USB—www.music-group.com/brand/behringer/ home
Mackie Onyx 1220i FireWire Production Mixer—http://mackie.com/ products/onyx-i-series

Podcast Hosting Services

audioBoom—https://audioboom.com
Blubrry—www.blubrry.com
Libsyn—www.libsyn.com
Podbean—https://podbean.com
SoundCloud—https://soundcloud.com/stream
Spreaker—www.spreaker.com

Remote Recording

JK Audio Broadcast Host—www.jkaudio.com/broadcast-host.htm
Skype—www.skype.com/en/
Zencastr—https://zencastr.com

Miscellaneous Equipment

CyberPower CP1350AVRLCD Intelligent LCD Series UPS 1350VA 810W AVR Mini-Tower—www.cyberpowersystems.com/product/ups/ cp1350avrlcd/
Heil Sound PRSM-B Shockmount (Black)—www.heilsound.com/amat eur/products/shock-mounts/prsm
Heil Sound PL2T Overhead Broadcast Boom—www.heilsound.com/ amateur/products/booms-and-hardware/pl2t
PreSonus HP4 4-Channel Compact Headphone Amplifier—www. presonus.com/products/hp4
PSM1 Shock Mount—www.rode.com/accessories/psm1
Rode PSA1 Studio Boom Arm—www.rode.com/accessories/psa1
XLR Cables—www.bhphotovideo.com/c/buy/XLR-to-XLR-Cables/ci/4174/ N/3992462205

Appendix C
It's All Journalism Questionnaire

This is an example of the email I send out before every *It's All Journalism* interview. I start out with a short introduction of the podcast and myself, followed by a phrase that sums up what the podcast is about. I try to change the phrase every few episodes. Then I introduce the guest, his or her area of expertise and what we're going to be discussing. The whole idea is to give the audience a point of reference to start with and then move quickly into the discussion. That's what people really want to hear.

I send about 10 questions to every guest. I try to cover a variety of topics, asking questions that elicit longer answers instead of just "yes" or "no." (For example: "Who do you see as your audience?" rather than "Your audience is people who want to record podcasts, right?")

Even though I always send 10 questions, I usually don't ask all of them. In fact, I rarely ask more than the first couple. However, the act of writing the questions and introduction helps me organize my thoughts about the interview. And if there's a lull in the conversation, I can always fall back on the list as a safety net.

Not every podcaster needs to send a list of questions like this to their guests, but it is worthwhile to at least let them know what you'd like to discuss ahead of time. It will make them more comfortable and give them a chance to prepare. You can still keep a few surprise questions in your pocket to spring on them or rely on the spontaneity of the moment to guide the discussion.

The trick for making any interview work is to be curious about what your guest does and listen to everything he or she says. Use your guest's answers as springboards for your questions.

It's All Journalism Email

Intro: Welcome to *It's All Journalism*, I'm Michael O'Connell here with another podcast about digital media and the people who make it. On the phone with me today is David Jackson, the founder of the School of Podcasting. He's going to share some tips about how to podcast.

Welcome, David. How are you doing?

—How did you get interested in podcasting?

—What was your goal in launching the School of Podcasting?

—How does the School of Podcasting work? (If I want to podcast, how can you help me? How do I get involved/sign up?)

—How would you describe the experience of running the School of Podcasting?

—Who do you see as your audience?

—What are the big mistakes that new podcasters tend to make?

—What advice would you give to someone starting out podcasting?

—What makes a successful podcast?

—How important is the technical side of production to the success of a podcast?

—What are your thoughts on using a podcasting platform like Libsyn, Blubrry, etc. to post your podcast? Advantages/disadvantages?

Bibliography

Abeid, Cesar (2016, July 7). Personal interview.

Alpert, Jessica (2016, June 17). Phone interview.

Augenstein, Neal (2016, May 16). Personal interview.

"Become a SoundCloud Pro" (2016). *SoundCloud.* [https://soundcloud.com/pro]

Campbell, Tiffany (2016, May 21). Phone interview.

Cochrane, Todd (2016, May 23). Phone interview.

Cope, Jordan (2016, July 7). Personal interview.

Coulter, Dave and Kat Jessup (2016, May 13). Personal interview.

Crawford, Jennifer and Timothy Trueheart (2016, June 6). Personal interview.

Curran, Chris (2016, Aug. 17). Phone interview.

Curry, Adam (2016, Aug. 16). Phone interview.

Delvac, Gina (2016, July 11). Phone interview.

DePrey, Nick (2016, July 8). "Minute by minute: How NPR uses listening data to make better radio." Podcast Movement presentation.

Dumas, John Lee (2016, July 14). Skype interview.

"Editing podcasts" (2016). Educational Technology for Healthcare Education, The University of Nottingham, United Kingdom. [http://nottingham.ac.uk/nmp/sonet/resources/podcasting/podcast_editing.html#metadata]

Franks, Dan (2016, Aug. 17). Phone interview.

Friedman, Lex (2013, July 22). "Apple: One billion iTunes podcast subscriptions and counting," *Macworld.* [www.macworld.com/article/2044958/apple-one-billion-itunes-podcast-subscriptions-and-counting.html]

Furlan, Julia (2016, June 10). Phone interview.

Glaser, Mark (2016, May 24). Phone interview.

Gluecksmann, Ernesto (2016, May 6). Personal interview.

Goldberg, Kevin (2016, June 2). Phone interview.

Goldberg, Kevin (2016, Oct. 27). Email interview.

"Guglielmo Marconi," *Wikipedia* [https://en.wikipedia.org/wiki/Guglielmo_Marconi]

Hesse, Monica (2016, Feb. 8). "'Serial' takes the stand: How a podcast became a character in its own narrative," *The Washington Post.* [www.washingtonpost.com/lifestyle/when-a-post-conviction-hearing-feels-like-a-sequel-the-weirdness-of-serial-back-on-the-stand/2016/02/08/b3782c60-2a49-48f7-9480-a34d-d9e07ab6_story.html]

Jackson, David (2016, Aug. 6). Skype interview.

Jacksonrao, Jay (2016, June 13). Skype interview.

Jurkowitz, MArk (2014, March 26). "The Losses in Legacy." State of the Media (blog), Pew Research Center. [http://www.journalism.org/2014/03/26/the-losses-in-legacy]

Kissimmee, Joey (2016, June 16). Phone interview.

Levi, Ran (2016, Aug. 2). Skype interview.

Levin, Adam (2016, July 5). Personal interview.

Lurie, Julia (2014, Sept. 19). " 'This American Life' channels 'True Detective' in a new podcast," *Mother Jones*. [www.motherjones.com/media/2014/09/ira-glass-sarah-koenig-julie-snyder-serial-podcast-this-american-life]

Mackey, Phil (2016, Sept. 13). Personal interview.

Martin, Shannon (2016, July 6). Personal interview.

Martin, Shannon (2016, June 8). "Where should I host my podcast?" *Podcasting Blog*. [https://podcastingblog.com/2016/06/08/where-should-i-host-my-podcast/]

Mayer, Laura (2016, June 8). Phone interview.

McKenna, Bill (2016, May 17). Phone interview.

"Media podcast hosting" (2017). *Blubrry*. [https://create.blubrry.com/manual/internet-media-hosting/]

Monaghan, Brendan (2016, June 14). Phone interview.

Mosel, Sarah van (2016, May 31). Phone interview.

"MP3 (MPEG Layer 3) tips for podcasting" (n.d.). *Blubrry*. [https://create.blubrry.com/manual/creating-podcast-media/audio/mp3-mpeg-layer-3-tips/]

Mulder, Steve (2016, Aug. 3). Phone interview.

Nelson, Steve (2016, June 2). Phone interview.

Nichols, Mary (2016, June 8). Skype interview.

Noorbakhsh, Zahra (2016, June 28). Phone interview.

Pattiz, Norman (2016, June 14). Phone interview.

Piazza, Anna (2016, July 7). Personal interview.

"Podcasts Connect help," *Apple*. [https://help.apple.com/itc/podcasts_connect/#/]

Poor, Nigel (2016, July 7). Personal interview.

Quirk, Vanessa (2015, Dec.). "Guide to podcasting," Tow Center for Digital Journalism, Columbia University. [http://towcenter.org/research/guide-to-podcasting/]

"RSS" (1999, March 15). *Wikipedia*. [https://en.wikipedia.org/wiki/RSS#cite_note-5]

Sachs, Adam (2016, Aug. 18). Phone interview.

Scharfenberg, Christa and Taki Telondis (2016, June 24). Phone interview.

"Serial/This American Life/Chicago Public Media," (2015, May 31). 74th Annual Peabody award winners. [www.peabodyawards.com/award-profile/serial]

Siuntres, John (2016, June 18). Phone interview.

Tan, Cheryl (2016, June 18). Skype interview.

Tan, Megan (2016, Aug. 4). Phone interview.

Tate, Tom (2016, July 6). Personal interview.

The Podcast Consumer 2016, Edison Research (2016, June). [edisonresearch.com/wp-content/uploads/2016/05/The-Podcast-Consumer-2016.pdf]

Thompson, Caitlin (2016, June 15). Phone interview.

Thorpe, Shawn (2015, Mar. 27). "iTunes album art spec goes up again," *Podcaster News.*
   [http://podcasternews.com/2015/03/27/itunes-album-art-spec-goes-up-again/]
Tobia, PJ (2016, June 16). Phone interview.
Walch, Robert (2016, May 23). Phone interview.
Webster, Tom (2016, June 20). Phone interview.
Winer, Dave (2000, Dec. 25). "RSS 0.92 specification," UserLand Software. Retrieved
   Oct. 31, 2006.

Resources

The following is a list of materials and websites that new podcasters might find useful. Some I used in my research, and others I came across while working on this book.

Books

"The Business of Podcasting" by Steve Lubetkin and Donna Papacosta [http://thebusinessofpodcasting.com]

"The Freedom Journal" by John Lee Dumas [https://thefreedomjournal.com]

"Podcasting: Do-It-Yourself Guide" by Todd Cochrane [www.amazon.com/Podcasting-Do-Yourself-Todd-Cochrane/dp/0764597787]

Conferences

DC PodFest—[www.dcpodfest.com]

Los Angeles Podcast Festival—[www.lapodfest.com]

Mid-Atlantic Podcast Conference—[http://podcastmidatlantic.com]

NYC PodFest—[http://nycpodfest.com]

Now Hear This Podcast Festival—[http://nowhearthisfest.com]

Philadelphia Podcast Festival—[www.phillypodfest.com]

Podcast Movement—[http://podcastmovement.com]

Educational Opportunities

Podcast Engineering School by Chris Curran [http://podcastengineeringschool.com]

The Podcaster's Paradise by John Lee Dumas [www.eofire.com/ppexplainer]

The School of Podcasting by David Jackson [http://schoolofpodcasting.com]

Useful Links

"Edison Research Hacks the Commuter Code: AM/FM listeners switch 22 times per commute," Edison Research (2016, April 7). [www.edisonresearch.com/edison-research-hacks-commuter-code-amfm-listeners-switch-22-times-per-commute/]

"EOFire's Income Reports," *EOFire (Entrepreneur on Fire)* podcast's monthly income reports. [www.eofire.com/income/]

"How to Measure Podcast Downloads," George Weiner, Whole Whale. [www. wholewhale.com/tips/measure-podcast-downloads/]

"The Podcast Consumer 2016," Edison Research (2016, May 26). [www.edison research.com/the-podcast-consumer-2016/]

"Podcast Industry Audience Rankings," Podtrac. [http://analytics.podtrac.com/ industry-rankings/]

"Podster Magazine," Shelf Media Group. [www.shelfmediagroup.com/pages/ podster.html]

"Public Radio Measurement Guidelines Version 1.1," Stephen Haptonstahl et al., Podcast Steering Group (2016, January). [bit.ly/podcastguidelines]

"Tow Center Report: Guide to Podcasting," Vanessa Quirk (2016, Dec. 7) [http:// towcenter.org/research/guide-to-podcasting/]

"Tutorial: Editing an Existing Audio File," Audacity. [http://manual.audacityteam. org/man/tutorial_editing_an_existing_file.html]

Podcasts

Advice! with Dave & Kat [www.advicepodcast.com]

Call Your Girlfriend [www.callyourgirlfriend.com]

The Carolyn and Joe Show [https://carolynandjoeshow.wordpress.com]

Curious Minds [www.cmpod.net]

Ear Hustle [https://www.earhustlesq.com/]

EOFire (Entrepreneur on Fire) [www.eofire.com]

FuseBox Radio Broadcast [http://fuseboxradio.com]

#GoodMuslimBadMuslim [www.goodmuslimbadmuslim.com]

The Hannah Graham Story [http://wtop.com/hannah-graham/]

Income Press [www.incomepress.com]

Internet Explorer [www.buzzfeed.com/iexplorer]

It's All Journalism [http://itsalljournalism.com]

The Jelly Vision Show [www.jellyvisionshowpodcast.com]

MediaShift [http://mediashift.org]

Millennial [www.millennialpodcast.org]

Modern Love [www.npr.org/podcasts/469516571/modern-love]

The Nerdpocalypse [www.thenerdpocalypse.com]

New Media Show [http://newmediashow.com]

No Agenda [www.noagendashow.com]

Not Another Podcast? [www.notanotherpodcastusa.com/about/]

The Podcast Engineering Show [http://fractalrecording.com/the-podcast-engineering-show/]

Project Management for the Masses [http://pmforthemasses.com]

Racquet [www.racquetmag.com/podcast/]

Reveal [www.revealnews.org]

School of Podcasting [www.schoolofpodcasting.libsyn.com]

Shortwave [www.podcastchart.com/podcasts/pbs-newshour-shortwave]

STANDOUT with Cheryl Tan [https://cheryltanmedia.com]

Through the Noise [http://throughthenoise.us/ernesto/]

Today in iOS [http://tii.libsyn.com]

Word Balloon with John Siuntres [https://wordballoonpodcast.wordpress.com]

Glossary

Ambient sound—In situations where a podcaster records an interview, she will also record a short piece of background sound in which no one is talking at the location. Then, when she edits together the interview and her narration, she will use the background sound as a bed under her narration to make the two pieces of audio—the narration and interview—sound as if they were recorded at the same time and in the same location.

Audience engagement—Rather than just promoting content, a podcaster participates in a two-way conversation with his audience through social media or other forms of marketing and interaction. The idea is to learn what his listeners like and to encourage them to share his podcast with their friends.

Audio player—Podcast listeners will use this web application or website plugin to listen to a piece of audio.

Cardioid microphone—Rather than an omnidirectional microphone, which records sound from all directions, a cardioid microphone records from only one direction. The advantage of this is the microphone focuses on one speaker and disregards the other noise in the room. With a cardioid microphone, though, the speaker needs to talk directly into the microphone at all times. If she turns her head or moves sideways, her voice will drop out of the microphone's range and will not be as loud or clear.

Closed-back headphones—A podcaster may use closed-back headphones to monitor the recording of a podcast. Because they have a solid back that completely covers the ears, this style of headphones prevents sound from "bleeding" out and being picked up by a microphone. Closed-back headphones can also be used during the editing process.

Compression—At the end of editing, a podcaster may compress the audio wave before he exports it. This will tighten up the distance between the high (loud) and low (quieter) ends of the audio wave, so that it sounds more consistent. Doing this means that the listener will not have to be constantly turning the volume up and down to hear the different voices.

Condenser microphone—A condenser is a very sensitive microphone usually found in a studio. It can have an omnidirectional or cardioid recording pattern. Because it is so sensitive, though, it needs to be in a place where outside noise is at a minimum and therefore performs best in a place like a studio.

Crowdfunding—A podcaster can raise money to launch or sustain a podcast by soliciting donations from his audience. This can be done as part of a one-time effort, such as a Kickstarter or Indiegogo campaign, or through ongoing support via PayPal or Patreon.

Data analytics—Media hosting services provide detailed information about the performance of the podcasts they host. This data can include the number of unique downloads, the platforms from which listeners accessed the episodes and what countries or cities the listeners are in. Some services also provide data on social media engagement.

Digital recorder—Any device that records audio digitally can be considered a digital recorder. However, the term usually refers to handheld or portable devices that record audio to internal memory or a removable memory card, such as an SD (Secure Digital) card. Digital recorders may have built-in microphones or jacks to plug in microphone cables. Usually, they allow audio to be recorded in either stereo or mono and in a variety of formats (MP3, .wav, etc.).

Download—In podcasting, a download refers to the audio file that a listener transfers to her listening device, which may be a desktop computer, smartphone, tablet or MP3 player. This is different from when a listener plays a podcast on a website audio player. In that case, no file is actually transferred from the website to the listener's device.

Dynamic insertion—Some podcasting networks have the ability to place commercials within the body of a podcast that is being hosted on their network's player. This differs from commercials that the podcaster actually records onto the audio file of a podcast, which will always be there in the audio. With dynamic insertion, the network can swap out commercials or even target commercials based on demographic information about the listener.

Dynamic microphone—Sturdier and less sensitive than a condenser microphone, a dynamic microphone can have an omnidirectional or cardioid recording pattern. It's a good choice for a beginning podcaster because it performs well in the field and does not require a full studio to record quality sound, although it can be used in a studio setting.

Earbuds—Earbuds are tiny headphones that are placed within the ear. Typically, they're used with portable listening devices, such as smartphones, MP3 players and tablets.

Email marketing—Rather than promoting content through social media or other means, a podcaster can encourage listeners to sign up for an email newsletter, which will not only let listeners know when new episodes are posted but also may include bonus content. This encourages an "exclusive club" feeling among subscribers. The email list can be used to send out surveys or solicit listener feedback. In addition, as the podcaster's email list grows, it provides a targeted list for the sale of merchandise, tickets or services to the podcast's audience.

Embeddable player—Some podcast hosting services, such as SoundCloud and Blubrry, provide a line of code that, when pasted into a website's HTML, creates a player so visitors can listen to a podcast episode directly from the website. This can be used instead of a website plugin that creates a player for the website.

Equalization—When editing, a podcaster may use equalization to remove the lower frequencies of a piece of audio so that the speakers' voices will be clearer to the listener.

FAQ—Creating a "Frequently Asked Questions" (FAQ) section on your website provides visitors with basic information about your podcast. This could include the podcast creators' iographies, a mission statement, sponsorship opportunities and a way for people to contact the podcast's creators.

Identifiable sound—When recording natural sound, a podcaster may seek out sounds that a listener will be able to easily recognize when they hear them, such as a baby crying or a school bell. These sounds are used instead of narration to set a scene and to place the listener in the location of the story.

Lavalier microphone—A podcaster can clip these small, omnidirectional microphones onto the clothing of a speaker to record an interview. A lavalier microphone may be wireless, or it may be hooked up to the podcaster's recording device via a wire.

Lead magnet—As part of a strategy to build an audience and grow an email list, you can create special podcast content, such as an interview that's accessible only to people who sign up on a website or a special report that's accessible only to people who provide their email address. For this strategy to work, the content needs to be something your audience will find useful or entertaining. The goal is to get your audience members to give you information in return for the content they desire. You can use this information, typically an email address, in your marketing efforts.

Mid-roll—A mid-roll refers to a commercial that is placed in the middle of a podcast, either by the podcaster recording it onto the audio track or through dynamic insertion. Mid-rolls are considered more effective than pre-rolls or post-rolls, which people tend to skip over. A listener driving a car, for example, may "endure" a short mid-roll rather than attempting to skip over it to get to the rest of the podcast.

Monetization—A podcaster may seek to raise money from her podcast through a variety of means, including advertising, sponsorships, events, merchandise sales and crowdfunding. The goal may be to make a profit or to raise enough money to sustain the production of the podcast. Monetization can also be done indirectly. In that case, the podcast is used primarily as a marketing device for a service that the podcaster provides, such as audio production, deejaying or special training.

MP3—When exporting her audio file, the podcaster can save it in MP3 (MPEG-1 Audio Layer III) format. This compact file is smaller than other media files and is therefore easier to distribute and download, making it an ideal format for audio podcasts.

Natural sound—When telling a story using natural sound, a podcaster may record different audio elements from the environment where the story takes place. Some of this audio may be identifiable sounds, while others may just be the general hubbub of the location. Natural sound may be used as a bed to narration or an interview, or it could just be a scene setter.

Omnidirectional microphone—Unlike a cardioid microphone, an omnidirectional microphone records sound equally from all directions. This can be useful in recording situations in which the microphone needs to be placed between multiple subjects. However, because the microphone records all sound equally, it will not distinguish between voices and other loud noises in the room.

Plugin—A plugin is an application that performs a particular function to enhance the content of a website. It could be an audio player, a photo gallery or a social media stream.

Podcast—A podcast is a collection of ideas recorded on audio or video that tells a story to educate and/or entertain an audience. The word can be used to describe a single episode or the entirety of the "show," meaning all the episodes and related content.

Podcast hosting service—Companies like Libsyn, Podbean and Blubrry provide media servers where podcasters can upload their audio or video content. These servers are robust enough to handle the large media files and traffic that podcasters may generate. These companies may also offer customers data analytics, websites and other services.

Podcast network—Companies like Acast, Midroll and PodcastOne are bringing together a variety of podcasts and creating networks similar to those found in traditional mass media. These podcast networks are marketing the combined audiences of all the podcasts under their umbrella, as well as the niche appeal of individual shows, to advertisers.

Podcatcher—A podcatcher is a computer program that downloads podcasts into an audio player via an RSS feed. Downcast, Overcast and Stitcher are among the many podcatchers currently available.

Post-roll—A post-roll refers to a commercial that is placed at the end of a podcast, either by the podcaster recording it onto the audio track or through dynamic insertion.

Pre-roll—A pre-roll refers to a commercial that is placed at the beginning of a podcast, either by the podcaster recording it onto the audio track or through dynamic insertion.

Really Simple Syndication (RSS)—RSS is an XML-based subscription service that allows individuals to subscribe to a website's content. Every time content is updated, the subscriber either receives a notice or the content is automatically downloaded to the subscriber's computer.

RSS feed—In podcasting, the RSS feed is the subscription code associated with a particular podcast. Listeners can subscribe to the RSS feed either through a podcatcher or through a media player, such as iTunes.

Shot list—Originating in journalistic photography, a shot list is a list of desired photographic subjects that a photographer jots down before going out on an assignment. The idea is to plan to take a variety of images that are visually interesting to tell the full story. When applied to podcasting, a shot list is an approach in which the podcaster plans out what audio elements she will need to tell her story. This may include collecting natural sound or tracking down certain interview subjects.

Shotgun microphone—A shotgun microphone is the long, thin microphone that you will sometimes see news reporters use. It's a cardioid microphone, which collects audio at one focused point while ignoring most surrounding noise.

Smartphone—Cellular phones such as the iPhone and Android devices are no longer just handheld communication devices; they're portable entertainment centers that provide up-to-the-minute news, access to social media and live-streaming audio and video. As such, they've become the primary way many people listen to podcasts. The iPhone has its Podcasts app, and Android users can download podcasts via Google Play and other podcatchers.

Social media—For podcasters, social media platforms like Facebook, Twitter and LinkedIn provide a place to promote content and interact with an audience. Because of the "social" aspect of the platforms, the most successful people are those who have a dialogue with their audience. They don't just broadcast the latest announcement; they share and listen to what their audience has to say.

Studio—A studio is the place where a podcaster records his episodes. It can be in a closed-off room with a large soundboard, multiple microphones and soundproof walls, or it can be a dining room table with a single microphone and a laptop computer. It's a quiet, controlled environment where the podcaster can record sound uninterrupted by outside noise or intrusion.

Universal Serial Bus (USB)—The interface between a computer or a peripheral device, such as a microphone or digital recorder. This allows you to record on your computer or download audio files for editing. An audio interface, for example, connects multiple microphones to a computer through a cable plugged into the computer's USB port.

Website—A website is a page on the World Wide Web where a podcaster can post content such as text stories, photos and hyperlinks to other websites. The website can also be a place where visitors can leave messages or listen to a podcast via an embeddable player or a built-in audio player.

Windscreen—A windscreen is a small piece of foam that a podcaster can place over the head of a microphone to deaden sharp sounds made in speech, usually referred to as "popping one's p's."

XLR cables—XLR cables are electronic cables used to connect audio or video equipment, such as microphones and mixers. They have cupped ends with three to seven metal pins (male) or holes (female).

Index

1/4-inch audio cables 32
"48 Hours" 81

Abeid, Cesar 110–11
Acast xxi, 13, 138–40
Adobe Audition 34–5, 98, 163
Adobe Premiere 163
ad servers 138–9
advertising: marketing plans 129–34
Advice! with Dave & Kat 172
affiliates 142
Ahmed, Tanzila "Taz" 48–9
The Airing of Grievances 51
AKG K52 closed-back headphones 164
album name, adding to audio files 106
Alpert, Jessica 56–7, 70, 74, 95–6
Althen, Blake 7–8, 92
Amazon Associates Program 145
ambient sound: definition of 174;
    including in podcasts 78–88
American Public Media 74, 87
Amoruso, Sophia 94
amplification slider (Audacity) 101
Amplify option (Audacity) 101
Appendipity 67–9, 113
artist name, adding to audio files 106
artwork: copyright for 159–61;
    uploading to iTunes 122
ASCAP, 154
Association of Alternative Newsmedia
    conference 79
Audacity 24, 163; editing audio with
    101–7; exporting audio from 105;
    importing audio into 100; workspace 99
audiences: audience engagement 145,
    174; measuring with data analytics
    135–8; relationship with podcasts 65;
    targeting 15–19; *see also* promotion
audioBoom 165

audio cables, selection of 31–2
audio editing: audio editing software
    98–107; episode elements 96–8;
    goals of 90–6; mono versus stereo
    100–1; theme music 103
audio editing software: Adobe Audition
    34–5, 98, 163; Audacity 24, 98–107;
    Cubase Studio 98; Ferrite 34–5;
    GarageBand 98; Hindenburg 98; Pro
    Tools 98; shopping guide 163–4
audio equipment *see* equipment
audio files: editing 98–107; exporting
    from Audacity 105; importing into
    Audacity 100
audio interfaces 36, 164
audio players: definition of 174;
    embeddable 176
audio production *see* studio setup
audio recording *see* recording process
audio tease 97
Audition (Adobe) 34–5, 98, 163
auditions, podcast episodes as 9–15
Augenstein, Neal 32–5, 81–7
authenticity 63–6, 93
AWeber Email Marketing 131

background interference, minimization
    of *see* studio setup
balanced cables 32
bandwidth, hosting services and 115
Beats headphones 31
Behringer Xenyx 1204 USB 165
best practices *see* podcasting best
    practices
bibliography 168–70
Bit Rate Mode option (Audacity) 105
Black on Black Cinema 50
Blubrry 23, 114–15, 118–19, 165
Blue Snowball 164

Blue Yeti USB microphone 35–6, 164
BMI 154
book recommendations 171
Bowers, Andy 52, 93
brand building 114
Broderick, Ryan 36–7
BuzzFeed 36, 92

cables (audio) 31–2
Call Your Girlfriend 41–2, 128–9, 172
Campbell, Tiffany 67, 70–1, 80–1,
  111–12
Capote, Truman 87
cardioid microphones 27–8, 174
Carlin, Dan 6
The Carolyn and Joe Show 172
Carpenter, Terrence 51
Center for Investigative Reporting 54
challenges of podcasting 2–5
Chuck Levin's Music Center 27
Clip Boundaries option (Audacity) 104
Cloherty, Megan 24
closed-back headphones 30–1, 174
Cochrane, Todd 2–3, 23, 100, 114,
  118–19
co-hosts, diversity of 57–9
Colbert, Stephen 7
"The Colbert Report" 7
"In Cold Blood" (Capote) 87
Collabspace events 143–4
commercials: mid-roll 176; PodcastOne
  model for xxi; post-roll 177; selling in
  podcasts 138–41
community building 146–7
compression 174
Compressor (Audacity) 105
comScore 137
condenser microphones 28–9, 174
conferences 171
content planning 40–1, 51; authenticity
  63–6; diversity of guests and co-hosts
  57–9; division of work 41–3; episode
  topics 43–4; story research and
  development 54–7; structure 44–53
conversation, podcasting as 57–9, 147
Cook, Tim 110
Cope, Jordan 146

copyright *see* music rights
Corcoran, Barbara 127
costs: Blubrry 118–19; headphones
  31; Libsyn 118; Podbean 119;
  SoundCloud 120–1; Spreaker 121
Coulter, Dave 49–50
Craft, Liz 52
Crawford, Jennifer 43–4, 58–9
Creative Commons licensing 158, 161
"Crosscurrents" (KALW) 45
crowdfunding 145–6, 175
Cubase Studio 98, 163
Culture Gabfest 94
Curious Minds 10–11, 172
Curran, Chris 22, 100, 106–7, 171
Curry, Adam 26, 146–7
Cursor Tool (Audacity) 101–2
Cut option (Audacity) 102
CyberPower CP1350AVRLCD
  Intelligent LCD Series UPS 1350VA
  810W AVR Mini-Tower 165

data analytics: definition of 175;
  measuring audiences with 135–8
DC PodFest 171
defamation 152
Delvac, Gina 41–3, 58, 128–9
democratization of media 58
Dense Pixels 51
DePrey, Nick 9–10
developer accounts, obtaining 118
development of content 54–7
digital recorders: definition of 175;
  shopping guide 164
diversity of guests and co-hosts 57–9
domain names, purchasing 113
donations, accepting 145
DoubleClick 136
downloads 175
Dumas, John Lee 5–6, 17–18, 68, 127,
  141–2, 171
Dvorak, John C. 146
dynamic insertion 175
dynamic microphones 28–9, 175

earbuds 175
Ear Hustle 44–7, 172

editing: audio editing software 98–107; authenticity and 93; episode elements 96–8; goals of 90–6; mono versus stereo 100–1; theme music 103
educational opportunities 171
Electronic Frontier Foundation Blogger's Rights 161
email: email marketing 133, 175; *It's All Journalism* questionnaire 166–7
embeddable players 176
Entrepreneur on Fire see EOFire
Envelope Tool (Audacity) 101, 103–4
environment, control of *see* studio setup
EOFire 5–6, 17–18, 68, 127, 141–2, 172
episodes: as auditions 9–15; elements of 96–8; length of 7–9; regularity of 5–7; time between 5–7; *see also* audio recording; content planning; editing
equalization 104–5, 176
Equalization tool (Audacity) 104–5
equipment 23–5; audio cables 31–2; audio interfaces 36; controlling environment for 25–7; failures of 23–5; foam windscreens 30; headphones 30–1; importance of 21–3; microphones 27–30; recording devices 32–7
Export Audio option (Audacity) 105
exporting Audacity files 105

Facebook: advertising on 132; podcast pages on 112; promoting podcasts on 128–9
"fair use" 156–8
Fallon, Jimmy 127
FAQs (Frequently Asked Questions) 176
Fast Forward button (Audacity) 99
Federal News Radio 28
feeds (RSS) 115–16, 178; *see also* hosting services
Ferriss, Tim 127
Ferrite 34–5, 163
file formats, MP3 105, 176
files *see* audio files
first episode, recording 74–6; *see also* content planning

"Fishko Files" (WNTC) 72
"The Flash," as representation of black family experience 59
Fletcher, Heald and Hildreth, PLC 151–2
Flynn, Pat 68
foam windscreens 30
format-driven podcasts 12
Franks, Dan 138
Free Music Archive 158
Friedman, Ann 42, 128
Furlan, Julia 36–7, 92
FuseBox Radio Broadcast 13–15, 172

GarageBand 98, 163
Gaye, Marvin 152–3
Geek News Central 3, 100
"Get Media Smart" 129–30
Girlboss Radio 94
Gladwell, Malcolm 72–3, 95
Glaser, Mark 143–5
glossary 174–9
Gluecksmann, Ernesto 7–8, 90–2
GoDaddy 113
GoFundMe 145
Goldberg, Kevin 151–9
Good Muslim, Bad Muslim 48–9, 172
Google Analytics 137
Google Play developer accounts 118
Graham, Hannah 81–2
growing podcasts *see* promotion
guests: asking questions of 73–4; diversity of 57–9; interviewing on location 78–88; listening to 73–4; researching in advance 67–73

"Hampton Roads Business Weekly" 129
The Hannah Graham Story 32, 81–7, 172
Happier with Gretchen Rubin 52–3, 94
Hardcore History 6
headphones: closed-back 30–1, 174; cost of 31; noise-canceling 31; open-back 30–1; selection of 30–1; shopping guide 164
Heil PR 40 Dynamic Studio Recording Microphone 164

Heil Sound PL2T Overhead Broadcast
    Boom 165
Heil Sound PRSM-B Shockmount
    165
Hindenburg 98, 164
hosting services: benefits of 109–10;
    Blubrry 23, 114–15, 118–19,
    165; definition of 177; Libsyn
    112, 115–18, 165; Podbean 115,
    119–20, 165; shopping guide 165;
    SoundCloud 22, 112, 115, 120–1,
    165; Spreaker 121, 165
hosts: diversity of 57–9; importance of
    11–12
"House of Cards" 87
HTML5 embeddable player 118

Idea Lab 143
identifiable sound 84–5, 176
IK Multimedia iRig Pro Audio/MIDI
    Interface 34–5, 164
importing audio into Audacity 100
Income Press 68, 113, 172
incorporation 159–61
Indiegogo 145
Instant Music Now 158
intellectual property rights see music
    rights
Internet Explorer 36, 172
interviews: asking questions in 73–4;
    audio teases from 97; editing 97–8;
    It's All Journalism questionnaire
    166–7; listening in 73–4; on location
    78–88; pre-interview research
    67–73; transcriptions of 97
introduction 97–8
iPhone see mobile technology
iRig 35
It's Advice! with Dave and Kat
    49–50
It's All Journalism xii; editing approach
    of 92–3; hosting service of 115–16;
    interviews on location 78–80; mono
    podcasting for 100–1; questionnaire
    166–7; "shot lists" for 66–7; storage
    requirements of 115; structure of
    97–8; website 172; WordPress pages
    for 112–13

iTunes: developer accounts 118;
    listing podcasts on 121–2; podcast
    subscriptions on 124;

Jackson, David 16, 124, 126–7, 167, 171
Jacksonrao, Jay 50–2, 58–9, 92, 142–3,
    160–1
The JellyVision Show 43, 58, 172
Jessup, Kat 49–50
JK Audio Broadcast Host 165
Join option (Audacity) 104
Jones, Daniel 56

KALW 45
Kickstarter 145
Kissimmee, Joey 67–9, 113

labor, division of 41–3
lavalier microphones 35–6, 176
lead magnets 176
Lee, Hae Min 82
legal issues: copyright royalties 152–3;
    defamation 152; "fair use" 156–8;
    incorporation 159–61; liability
    159–61; online music services
    158–9; public domain 158; releases
    155–6; responsibilities of podcasters
    151–2; statutory licenses 154–5
length of episodes 7–9
Lennon, John 152–3
Levi, Ran 10–11
Levin, Adam 27–32, 35–6
Levin, Chuck 27
liability issues 159–61
Liberated Syndication see Libsyn
Libsyn 112, 115–18, 165
licenses, statutory 154–5
limited liability corporation (LLC)
    160–1, 162
LinkedIn, promoting podcasts on
    128–9
listenership see audiences
listening to guests 73–4
LLC (limited liability corporation)
    160–1, 162
location, recording on 78–88
Look Forward 51
Los Angeles Podcast Festival 171

Mackey, Phil 40
Mackey & Judd radio show 40
Mackie Onyx 1220i FireWire
    Production Mixer 165
marketing: email marketing 175;
    marketing plans 129–34
Martin, Shannon 115–16, 119
Matthew, Jesse 82
M-Audio M-Track MKII Two-Channel
    USB Audio Interface 164
Mayer, Laura 2, 8–9, 52–3, 72–3, 93–5
McCartney, Paul 152–3
McKenna, Bill 63–6, 145, 161
"On the Media" (WNYC) 72
media coverage, promoting podcasts
    with 133–4
media law *see* legal issues
MediaShift 143–4, 172
The Men with the Golden Tongues 51
merchandise, selling 145
metadata, adding to audio files 106
Metadata option (Audacity) 106
metrics 135–8
microphone icon (Audacity) 99
microphones: cardioid 27–8, 174;
    condenser 28–9, 174; dynamic
    28–9, 175; lavalier 35–6, 176;
    omnidirectional 28–9, 177; selection
    of 27–30; shopping guide 164–5;
    shotgun 178; shotgun microphones
    28; windscreens 30
Mid-Atlantic Podcast Conference 171
mid-roll 138, 176
Midroll Media 2, 9, 138, 140–1
Millennial 17, 172
Mixergy 68
mixers 165
mobile technology: adoption of
    xix; impact on podcasts xxvii; as
    recording device 33–5
Modern Love 11–12, 56–7, 70–1, 95–6,
    172
Monaghan, Brendan 6–7, 127, 135
monetization: Amazon Associates
    Program 145; audience engagement
    events 145; commercial advertising
    138–41; community building 146–7;
    crowdfunding 145–6; definition of

176; *EOFire* case study 141–2; *The
    Nerdpocalypse* case study 142–3;
    PayPal donations 145; premiere
    content 142–3; sponsorships 138–41,
    143–4; *see also* promotion
mono files 100–1
The Morning Announcements 16
Mosel, Sarah van 13, 139–40
MP3 format 105, 176
Mulder, Steve 136–7
music, adding to podcasts 103
music rights: copyright royalties
    152–3; "fair use" 156–8; liability
    issues 159–61; online music services
    158–9; public domain 158; releases
    155–6; responsibilities of podcasters
    151–2; statutory licenses 154–5
MXL 990 USB 164

names for podcasts, selection of 15–17
natural conversation, editing for 91–2
natural sound 78–88, 177
Nelson, Steve 74, 87–8
NEO Sounds 158
The Nerdpocalypse 50–2, 58–9, 92,
    142–3, 172
The New Media Show 3, 172
news coverage, promoting podcasts
    through 134
Nichols, Mary 13–15, 58–9
Nielsen 137
No Agenda 146, 172
noise-canceling headphones 31
nonprofits, forming 161
Noorbakhsh, Zahra 48
Not Another Podcast? 63–6, 145, 161,
    172
not-for-profits, forming 161
No Time to Bleed 51
Notopoulos, Katie 36–7
Now Hear This Podcast Festival 171
NPR 74, 87, 136
NPR One 9–10
NYC PodFest 171

omnidirectional microphones 28–9,
    177
online stores 145

open-back headphones 30–1
Opuzz 158
outro tease 98
Overcast 116

Panoply 2, 6–7; data analytics and
    135; editing approach of 93–5;
    episode preparation 72–3; podcast
    advertising 138; promotion of 127;
    structure of 52
Paste option (Audacity) 102
Patreon 145–6
Pause button (Audacity) 99
Payne, Micah 51
PayPal donations 145
"PBS NewsHour" 96–7
Philadelphia Podcast Festival 171
photographs, copyright for 159–61
Piazza, Anna 121
Pike Place Market, podcast recorded at
    80–1
Pinterest, promoting podcasts on 129
planning episodes see audio recording;
    content planning
Play button (Audacity) 99
players see audio players
Plotz, David 7
plugins 113, 177
Podbean 115, 119–20, 165
podCast 411 116
podcast editing see editing
Podcast Engineering School 171
The Podcast Engineering Show 22, 100,
    172
podcast episodes see episodes
The Podcaster's Paradise 171
podcast hosting see hosting services
podcasting best practices 1–2;
    commitment to work 2–5; episode
    length 7–9; episodes as auditions
    9–15; podcast names 15–17; regular
    episodes 5–7; target audience 15–19
Podcasting Legal Guide 162
podcasting schools 171
podcast listenership see audiences
Podcast Movement 171
podcast networks 177
PodcastOne 138

podcast promotion see promotion
podcasts, definition of 177
podcast subscriptions, growth of 124
podcast teams: division of work 41–3;
    producers 41–3
podcast websites 172–3
podcatchers 177
Podquest contest 47
Podtrac 138
Political Gabfest 7, 94
Poor, Nigel 44–7
"popping your p's" 30
post-roll 138, 177
PowerPress 114
pre-interview research 67–73
Premiere (Adobe) 163
premiere content 142–3
pre-roll 138
PreSonus AudioBox iTwo 164
PreSonus HP4 4-Channel Compact
    Headphone Amplifier 165
pricing plans: Blubrry 118–19; Libsyn
    118; Podbean 119; SoundCloud
    120–1; Spreaker 121
Prince, death of 63–4
producers 41–3
project management 110–11
Project Management for the Masses
    110–11, 172
promotion 124–5; community building
    146–7; data analytics 135–8; email
    marketing 133; marketing plans
    129–34; media coverage 133–4;
    relationship building 126–8; social
    media 128–9; see also monetization
Pro Tools 98, 164
PRX (Public Radio Exchange) 54
PSM1 Shock Mount 165
public domain 158
Public Radio Exchange (PRX) 54

Quality option (Audacity) 105–6
questionnaire (It's All Journalism)
    166–7
questions, asking 73–4

Racquet 172
Radiotopia 47

Raw Voice 2–4, 114
Really Simple Syndication: definition of 177; feeds 178; RSS feeds 115–16, 178; *see also* hosting services
Record button (Audacity) 99
recording devices, selection of 32–7
recording process 62; ambient sound 78–88; asking questions during 73–4; authenticity in 63–6; checking recording quality 76; first episode 74–6; listening during 73–4; planning 66–7; pre-interview research 67–73; *see also* studio setup
recording quality, checking 76
recording setup *see* studio setup
regular episodes, producing 5–7
relationship building 126–8
releases 155–6
remote recording 165
resources 171–3
Reveal 54–6, 172
Revisionist History 72, 95
Rewind button (Audacity) 99
Rich Site Summary *see* Really Simple Syndication
Rode Procaster Broadcast Dynamic Vocal Microphone 164
Rode PSA1 Studio Boom Arm 165
Rous, Jack 51
royalties 152–3
RSS (Really Simple Syndication) *see* Really Simple Syndication
Rubin, Gretchen 53, 94

Sachs, Adam 2, 9, 140–1
San Quentin State Prison, podcast recorded at 44–7
Scharfenberg, Christa 54–6
The School of Podcasting 16, 171–2
schools (podcasting) 171
Seattle's Pike Place Market, podcast recorded at 80–1
Sennheiser e 835 microphone 165
Serial 6, 81–7, 125
SESAC 154
shopping guide 163–5
Shortwave 96–7, 172

shotgun microphones 28, 178
shot lists 67, 178
show credits 98
Simons, Brett 63–6
sincerity 65
Sisson, Natalie 68
Siuntres, John 125
Skype 3, 26, 37, 48, 79, 126, 165
Slate magazine 7, 94
The Smart Passive Income Blog 68
smartphones 178; *see also* mobile technology
Snyder, Julie 87
social media: definition of 178; promoting podcasts on 128–9
Society for News Design conference 79
software *see* audio editing software
Sony MDR7506 Professional large diaphragm headphones 164
Sony Vegas Pro 164
sound: identifiable 84–5, 176; natural 78–88, 177
SoundCloud 22, 112, 115, 120–1, 165
Song Exploder 12
Sow, Aminatou 42, 128
Split option (Audacity) 104
sponsorships 138–41, 143–4
Spreaker 121, 165
Squarespace 112
STANDOUT with Cheryl Tan 129–31, 172
statutory licenses 154–5
stereo files 100–1
Stereo Track to Mono option (Audacity) 101
Stitcher 116
Stop button (Audacity) 99
storage size, hosting services and 115
stores (online) 145
story research and development 54–7
structure: as launching pad for new directions 52–3; working within 44–52
Studio Projects B1 165
studio setup 21–3; audio cables 31–2; audio interfaces 36; challenges of 23–5; controlling environment

for 25–7; foam windscreens 30;
    headphones 30–1; microphones
    27–30; recording devices 32–7;
    "studio" defined 178
subscriptions, growth of 124
The Suitcase Entrepreneur 68
sustaining podcasts *see* promotion

Tan, Cheryl 129–31, 134
Tan, Megan 4–5, 17
target audience, identifying 15–19
Tascam digital recorders 32, 164
Tate, Tom 131
tease elements: audio tease 97; outro
    tease 98
Telondis, Taki 54–6
tenets of podcasting *see* podcasting best
    practices
text, copyright laws for 159–61
theme music, adding to podcast
    103
This Week in Startups 42
Thompson, Caitlin 11–13
Through the Noise 7–8, 90–2, 172
time between episodes 5–7
Time Shift Tool (Audacity) 103–4
TNP Studios 142–3, 160
Tobia, PJ 96–7
Today in iOS 172
topics, selection of 12–13, 43–4
Track option (Audacity) 101–7
track title, adding to audio files 106
transcriptions of interviews 97
transitions, identifiable sound in
    84–5
Trueheart, Tim 43–4
Tumblr 112
Twitter, advertising on 132

unbalanced cables 32
Universal Serial Bus (USB) 178

Vaynerchuk, Gary 127
Vele, Mike 81

Walch, Robert 116–17
Warner, Andrew 68
WBUR 67, 70, 80, 111
websites: articles 171–2; audio editing
    software 163–4; audio interfaces
    164; books 171; conferences 171;
    definition of 178; digital recorders
    164; educational opportunities
    171; headphones 164; microphones
    164–5; mixers 165; music rights
    161–2; podcast hosting services 165;
    podcasts 172–3; posting podcasts to
    109; remote recording 165; selection
    of 110–14; WordPress 112–14
Williams, Antwan 44–7
Williams, Troy 45
windscreens 30
Woods, Earlonne 44–7
Word Balloon 125, 172
WordPress sites, building 112–14
workload, division of 41–3
workspace (Audacity) 99
WTOP 81
WVWC 63

XLR cables 32, 165

"Yesterday" (The Beatles) 152–3

Zencastr 165
Zoom digital recorders 32, 164
Zoom tools (Audacity) 102